P9-CMD-491

SYMPOSIUM

PLATO

Translated by
BENJAMIN JOWETT

Originally published in 1892, this translation of Plato's work is in the public domain. No copyright claim is made with respect to public domain work.

This edition reflects minor editorial revisions to the original text.

INTRODUCTION

Of all the works of Plato the Symposium is the most perfect in form, and may be truly thought to contain more than any commentator has ever dreamed of; or, as Goethe said of one of his own writings, more than the author himself knew. For in philosophy as in prophecy glimpses of the future may often be conveyed in words which could hardly have been understood or interpreted at the time when they were uttered (compare Symp.)—which were wiser than the writer of them meant, and could not have been expressed by him if he had been interrogated about them. Yet Plato was not a mystic, nor in any degree affected by the Eastern influences which afterwards overspread the Alexandrian world. He was not an enthusiast or a sentimentalist, but one who aspired only to see reasoned truth, and whose thoughts are clearly explained in his language. There is no foreign element either of Egypt or of Asia to be found in his writings. And more than any other Platonic work the Symposium is Greek both in style and subject, having a beauty 'as of a statue,' while the companion Dialogue of the Phaedrus is marked by a sort of Gothic irregularity. More too than in any other of his Dialogues, Plato is emancipated from former philosophies. The genius of Greek art seems to triumph over the traditions of Pythagorean, Eleatic, or Megarian systems, and 'the old quarrel of poetry and philosophy' has at least a superficial reconcilement. (Rep.)

An unknown person who had heard of the discourses in praise of love spoken by Socrates and others at the banquet of Agathon is desirous of having an authentic account of them, which he thinks that he can obtain from Apollodorus, the same excitable, or rather 'mad' friend of Socrates, who is afterwards introduced in the Phaedo. He had imagined that the discourses were recent. There he is mistaken: but they are still fresh in the memory of his informant, who had just been repeating them to Glaucon, and is quite prepared to have another rehearsal of them in a walk from the Piraeus to Athens. Although he had not been present himself, he had heard them from the best authority. Aristodemus, who is described as having been in past times a humble but inseparable attendant of Socrates, had reported them to him (compare Xen. Mem.).

The narrative which he had heard was as follows:—

Aristodemus meeting Socrates in holiday attire, is invited by him to a banquet at the house of Agathon, who had been sacrificing in thanksgiving for his tragic victory on the day previous. But no sooner has he entered the house than he finds that he is alone; Socrates has stayed behind in a fit of abstraction, and does not appear until the banquet is half over. On his appearing he and the host jest a little; the question is then asked by Pausanias, one of the guests, 'What shall they do about drinking? as they had been all

well drunk on the day before, and drinking on two successive days is such a bad thing.' This is confirmed by the authority of Eryximachus the physician, who further proposes that instead of listening to the flute-girl and her 'noise' they shall make speeches in honour of love, one after another, going from left to right in the order in which they are reclining at the table. All of them agree to this proposal, and Phaedrus, who is the 'father' of the idea, which he has previously communicated to Eryximachus, begins as follows:
—

He descants first of all upon the antiquity of love, which is proved by the authority of the poets; secondly upon the benefits which love gives to man. The greatest of these is the sense of honour and dishonour. The lover is ashamed to be seen by the beloved doing or suffering any cowardly or mean act. And a state or army which was made up only of lovers and their loves would be invincible. For love will convert the veriest coward into an inspired hero.

And there have been true loves not only of men but of women also. Such was the love of Alcestis, who dared to die for her husband, and in recompense of her virtue was allowed to come again from the dead. But Orpheus, the miserable harper, who went down to Hades alive, that he might bring back his wife, was mocked with an apparition only, and the gods afterwards contrived his death as the punishment of his cowardliness. The love of Achilles, like that of Alcestis, was courageous and true; for he was willing to avenge his lover Patroclus, although he knew that his own death would immediately follow: and the gods, who honour the love of the beloved above that of the lover, rewarded him, and sent him to the islands of the blest.

Pausanias, who was sitting next, then takes up the tale:— He says that Phaedrus should have distinguished the heavenly love from the earthly, before he praised either. For there are two loves, as there are two Aphrodites—one the daughter of Uranus, who has no mother and is the elder and wiser goddess, and the other, the daughter of Zeus and Dione, who is popular and common. The first of the two loves has a noble purpose, and delights only in the intelligent nature of man, and is faithful to the end, and has no shadow of wantonness or lust. The second is the coarser kind of love, which is a love of the body rather than of the soul, and is of women and boys as well as of men. Now the actions of lovers vary, like every other sort of action, according to the manner of their performance. And in different countries there is a difference of opinion about male loves. Some, like the Boeotians, approve of them; others, like the Ionians, and most of the barbarians, disapprove of them; partly because they are aware of the political dangers which ensue from them, as may be seen in the instance of Harmodius and Aristogeiton. At Athens and Sparta there is an apparent contradiction about them. For at times they are encouraged, and then the lover is allowed to play all sorts of fantastic tricks; he may swear and forswear himself (and 'at lovers' perjuries they say Jove laughs'); he may be a servant, and lie on a mat at the door of his love, without any loss of character; but there are also times when elders look grave and guard their young relations, and personal remarks are made. The truth is that some of these loves are disgraceful and others honourable. The vulgar love of the body which takes wing and flies away when the bloom of youth is over, is disgraceful, and so is the interested love of power or wealth;

but the love of the noble mind is lasting. The lover should be tested, and the beloved should not be too ready to yield. The rule in our country is that the beloved may do the same service to the lover in the way of virtue which the lover may do to him.

A voluntary service to be rendered for the sake of virtue and wisdom is permitted among us; and when these two customs—one the love of youth, the other the practice of virtue and philosophy—meet in one, then the lovers may lawfully unite. Nor is there any disgrace to a disinterested lover in being deceived: but the interested lover is doubly disgraced, for if he loses his love he loses his character; whereas the noble love of the other remains the same, although the object of his love is unworthy: for nothing can be nobler than love for the sake of virtue. This is that love of the heavenly goddess which is of great price to individuals and cities, making them work together for their improvement.

The turn of Aristophanes comes next; but he has the hiccough, and therefore proposes that Eryximachus the physician shall cure him or speak in his turn. Eryximachus is ready to do both, and after prescribing for the hiccough, speaks as follows:—

He agrees with Pausanias in maintaining that there are two kinds of love; but his art has led him to the further conclusion that the empire of this double love extends over all things, and is to be found in animals and plants as well as in man. In the human body also there are two loves; and the art of medicine shows which is the good and which is the bad love, and persuades the body to accept the good and reject the bad, and reconciles conflicting elements and makes them friends. Every art, gymnastic and husbandry as well as medicine, is the reconciliation of opposites; and this is what Heracleitus meant, when he spoke of a harmony of opposites: but in strictness he should rather have spoken of a harmony which succeeds opposites, for an agreement of disagreements there cannot be. Music too is concerned with the principles of love in their application to harmony and rhythm. In the abstract, all is simple, and we are not troubled with the twofold love; but when they are applied in education with their accompaniments of song and metre, then the discord begins. Then the old tale has to be repeated of fair Urania and the coarse Polyhymnia, who must be indulged sparingly, just as in my own art of medicine care must be taken that the taste of the epicure be gratified without inflicting upon him the attendant penalty of disease.

There is a similar harmony or disagreement in the course of the seasons and in the relations of moist and dry, hot and cold, hoar frost and blight; and diseases of all sorts spring from the excesses or disorders of the element of love. The knowledge of these elements of love and discord in the heavenly bodies is termed astronomy, in the relations of men towards gods and parents is called divination. For divination is the peacemaker of gods and men, and works by a knowledge of the tendencies of merely human loves to piety and impiety. Such is the power of love; and that love which is just and temperate has the greatest power, and is the source of all our happiness and friendship with the gods and with one another. I dare say that I have omitted to mention many things which you, Aristophanes, may supply, as I perceive that you are cured of the hiccough.

Aristophanes is the next speaker:—

He professes to open a new vein of discourse, in which he begins by treating of the origin of human nature. The sexes were originally three, men, women, and the union of the two; and they were made round—having four hands, four feet, two faces on a round neck, and the rest to correspond. Terrible was their strength and swiftness; and they were essaying to scale heaven and attack the gods. Doubt reigned in the celestial councils; the gods were divided between the desire of quelling the pride of man and the fear of losing the sacrifices. At last Zeus hit upon an expedient. Let us cut them in two, he said; then they will only have half their strength, and we shall have twice as many sacrifices. He spake, and split them as you might split an egg with an hair; and when this was done, he told Apollo to give their faces a twist and re-arrange their persons, taking out the wrinkles and tying the skin in a knot about the navel. The two halves went about looking for one another, and were ready to die of hunger in one another's arms. Then Zeus invented an adjustment of the sexes, which enabled them to marry and go their way to the business of life. Now the characters of men differ accordingly as they are derived from the original man or the original woman, or the original man-woman. Those who come from the man-woman are lascivious and adulterous; those who come from the woman form female attachments; those who are a section of the male follow the male and embrace him, and in him all their desires centre. The pair are inseparable and live together in pure and manly affection; yet they cannot tell what they want of one another. But if Hephaestus were to come to them with his instruments and propose that they should be melted into one and remain one here and hereafter, they would acknowledge that this was the very expression of their want. For love is the desire of the whole, and the pursuit of the whole is called love. There was a time when the two sexes were only one, but now God has halved them,—much as the Lacedaemonians have cut up the Arcadians,—and if they do not behave themselves he will divide them again, and they will hop about with half a nose and face in basso relievo. Wherefore let us exhort all men to piety, that we may obtain the goods of which love is the author, and be reconciled to God, and find our own true loves, which rarely happens in this world. And now I must beg you not to suppose that I am alluding to Pausanias and Agathon (compare Protag.), for my words refer to all mankind everywhere.

Some raillery ensues first between Aristophanes and Eryximachus, and then between Agathon, who fears a few select friends more than any number of spectators at the theatre, and Socrates, who is disposed to begin an argument. This is speedily repressed by Phaedrus, who reminds the disputants of their tribute to the god. Agathon's speech follows:—

He will speak of the god first and then of his gifts: He is the fairest and blessedest and best of the gods, and also the youngest, having had no existence in the old days of Iapetus and Cronos when the gods were at war. The things that were done then were done of necessity and not of love. For love is young and dwells in soft places,—not like Ate in Homer, walking on the skulls of men, but in their hearts and souls, which are soft enough. He is all flexibility and grace, and his habitation is among the flowers, and he cannot do or suffer wrong; for all men serve and obey him of their own free will, and where there is love there is obedience, and where obedience, there is justice; for none can be wronged of his own free will. And he is temperate as well as just, for he is the ruler of the desires, and if he rules them he must be temperate. Also he is courageous, for he is the conqueror of the lord of war. And he is wise too; for he is a poet, and the author of poesy in others. He created the animals; he is the inventor of the arts; all the gods are his subjects; he is the fairest and best himself, and the cause of what is fairest and best in others; he makes men to be of one mind at a banquet, filling them with affection and emptying them of disaffection; the pilot, helper, defender, saviour of men, in whose footsteps let every man follow, chanting a strain of love. Such is the discourse, half playful, half serious, which I dedicate to the god.

The turn of Socrates comes next. He begins by remarking satirically that he has not understood the terms of the original agreement, for he fancied that they meant to speak the true praises of love, but now he finds that they only say what is good of him, whether true or false. He begs to be absolved from speaking falsely, but he is willing to speak the truth, and proposes to begin by questioning Agathon. The result of his questions may be summed up as follows:—

Love is of something, and that which love desires is not that which love is or has; for no man desires that which he is or has. And love is of the beautiful, and therefore has not the beautiful. And the beautiful is the good, and therefore, in wanting and desiring the beautiful, love also wants and desires the good. Socrates professes to have asked the same questions and to have obtained the same answers from Diotima, a wise woman of Mantinea, who, like Agathon, had spoken first of love and then of his works. Socrates, like Agathon, had told her that Love is a mighty god and also fair, and she had shown him in return that Love was neither, but in a mean between fair and foul, good and evil, and not a god at all, but only a great demon or intermediate power (compare the speech of Eryximachus) who conveys to the gods the prayers of men, and to men the commands of the gods.

Socrates asks: Who are his father and mother? To this Diotima replies that he is the son of Plenty and Poverty, and partakes of the nature of both, and is full and starved by turns. Like his mother he is poor and squalid, lying on mats at doors (compare the speech of Pausanias); like his father he is bold and strong, and full of arts and resources. Further, he is in a mean between ignorance and knowledge:—in this he resembles the philosopher who is also in a mean between the wise and the ignorant. Such is the nature of Love, who is not to be confused with the beloved.

But Love desires the beautiful; and then arises the question, What does he desire of the beautiful? He desires, of course, the possession of the beautiful;—but what is given by that? For the beautiful let us substitute the good, and we have no difficulty in seeing the possession of the good to be happiness, and Love to be the desire of happiness, although the meaning of the word has been too often confined to one kind of love. And Love desires not only the good, but the everlasting possession of the good. Why then is there all this flutter and excitement about love? Because all men and women at a certain age are desirous of bringing to the birth.

And love is not of beauty only, but of birth in beauty; this is the principle of immortality in a mortal creature. When beauty approaches, then the conceiving power is benign and diffuse; when foulness, she is averted and morose.

But why again does this extend not only to men but also to animals? Because they too have an instinct of immortality. Even in the same individual there is a perpetual succession as well of the parts of the material body as of the thoughts and desires of the mind; nay, even knowledge comes and goes. There is no sameness of existence, but the new mortality is always taking the place of the old. This is the reason why parents love their children—for the sake of immortality; and this is why men love the immortality of fame. For the creative soul creates not children, but conceptions of wisdom and virtue, such as poets and other creators have invented. And the noblest creations of all are those of legislators, in honour of whom temples have been raised. Who would not sooner have these children of the mind than the ordinary human ones? (Compare Bacon's Essays, 8:—'Certainly the best works and of greatest merit for the public have proceeded from the unmarried or childless men; which both in affection and means have married and endowed the public.')

I will now initiate you, she said, into the greater mysteries; for he who would proceed in due course should love first one fair form, and then many, and learn the connexion of them; and from beautiful bodies he should proceed to beautiful minds, and the beauty of laws and institutions, until he perceives that all beauty is of one kindred; and from institutions he should go on to the sciences, until at last the vision is revealed to him of a single science of universal beauty, and then he will behold the everlasting nature which is the cause of all, and will be near the end. In the contemplation of that supreme being of love he will be purified of earthly leaven, and will behold beauty, not with the bodily eye, but with the eye of the mind, and will bring forth true creations of virtue and wisdom, and be the friend of God and heir of immortality.

Such, Phaedrus, is the tale which I heard from the stranger of Mantinea, and which you may call the encomium of love, or what you please.

The company applaud the speech of Socrates, and Aristophanes is about to say something, when suddenly a band of revellers breaks into the court, and the voice of Alcibiades is heard asking for Agathon. He is led in drunk, and welcomed by Agathon, whom he has come to crown with a garland. He is placed on a couch at his side, but suddenly, on recognizing Socrates, he starts up, and a sort of conflict is carried on between them, which Agathon is requested to appease. Alcibiades then insists that they shall drink, and has a large wine-cooler filled, which he first empties himself, and then fills again and passes on to Socrates. He is informed of the nature of the entertainment; and is ready to join, if only in the character of a drunken and disappointed lover he may be allowed to sing the praises of Socrates:—

He begins by comparing Socrates first to the busts of Silenus, which have images of the gods inside them; and, secondly, to Marsyas the flute-player. For Socrates produces the same effect with the voice which Marsyas did with the flute. He is the great speaker and enchanter who ravishes the souls of men; the convincer of hearts too, as he has convinced Alcibiades, and made him ashamed of his mean and miserable life. Socrates at one time seemed about to fall in love with him; and he thought that he would thereby gain a wonderful opportunity of receiving lessons of wisdom. He narrates the failure of his design. He has suffered agonies from him, and is at his wit's end. He then proceeds to mention some other particulars of the life of Socrates; how they were at Potidaea together, where Socrates showed his superior powers of enduring cold and fatigue; how on one occasion he had stood for an entire day and night absorbed in reflection amid the wonder of the spectators; how on another occasion he had saved Alcibiades' life; how at the battle of Delium, after the defeat, he might be seen stalking about like a pelican, rolling his eyes as Aristophanes had described him in the Clouds. He is the most wonderful of human beings, and absolutely unlike anyone but a satyr. Like the satyr in his language too; for he uses the commonest words as the outward mask of the divinest truths.

When Alcibiades has done speaking, a dispute begins between him and Agathon and Socrates. Socrates piques Alcibiades by a pretended affection for Agathon. Presently a band of revellers appears, who introduce disorder into the feast; the sober part of the company, Eryximachus, Phaedrus, and others, withdraw; and Aristodemus, the follower of Socrates, sleeps during the whole of a long winter's night. When he wakes at cockcrow the revellers are nearly all asleep. Only Socrates, Aristophanes, and Agathon hold out; they are drinking from a large goblet, which they pass round, and Socrates is explaining to the two others, who are half-asleep, that the genius of tragedy is the same as that of comedy, and that the writer of tragedy ought to be a writer of comedy also. And first Aristophanes drops, and then, as the day is dawning, Agathon. Socrates, having laid them to rest, takes a bath and goes to his daily avocations until the evening. Aristodemus follows.

If it be true that there are more things in the Symposium of Plato than any commentator has dreamed of, it is also true that many things have been imagined which are not really to be found there. Some writings hardly admit of a more distinct interpretation than a musical composition; and every reader may form his own accompaniment of thought or feeling to the strain which he hears. The Symposium of Plato is a work of this character, and can with difficulty be rendered in any words but the writer's own. There are so many half-lights and cross-lights, so much of the colour of mythology, and of the manner of sophistry adhering—rhetoric and poetry, the playful and the serious, are so subtly intermingled in it, and vestiges of old philosophy so curiously blend with germs of future knowledge, that agreement among interpreters is not to be expected. The expression 'poema magis putandum quam comicorum poetarum,' which has been applied to all the writings of Plato, is especially applicable to the Symposium.

The power of love is represented in the Symposium as running through all nature and all being: at one end descending to animals and plants, and attaining to the highest vision of truth at the other. In an age when man was seeking for an expression of the world around him, the conception of love greatly affected him. One of the first distinctions of language and of mythology was that of gender; and at a later period the ancient physicist, anticipating modern science, saw, or thought that he saw, a sex in plants; there were elective affinities among the elements, marriages of earth and heaven. (Aesch. Frag. Dan.) Love became a mythic personage whom philosophy, borrowing from poetry, converted into an efficient cause of creation. The traces of the existence of love, as of number and figure, were everywhere discerned; and in the Pythagorean list of opposites male and female were ranged side by side with odd and even, finite and infinite.

But Plato seems also to be aware that there is a mystery of love in man as well as in nature, extending beyond the mere immediate relation of the sexes. He is conscious that the highest and noblest things in the world are not easily severed from the sensual desires, or may even be regarded as a spiritualized form of them. We may observe that Socrates himself is not represented as originally unimpassioned, but as one who has overcome his passions; the secret of his power over others partly lies in his passionate but self-controlled nature. In the Phaedrus and Symposium love is not merely the feeling usually so called, but the mystical contemplation of the beautiful and the good. The same passion which may wallow in the mire is capable of rising to the loftiest heights—of penetrating the inmost secret of philosophy. The highest love is the love not of a person, but of the highest and purest abstraction. This abstraction is the far-off heaven on which the eye of the mind is fixed in fond amazement. The unity of truth, the consistency of the warring elements of the world, the enthusiasm for knowledge when first beaming upon mankind, the relativity of ideas to the human mind, and of the human mind to ideas, the faith in the invisible, the adoration of the eternal nature, are all included, consciously or unconsciously, in Plato's doctrine of love.

The successive speeches in praise of love are characteristic of the speakers, and contribute in various degrees to the final result; they are all designed to prepare the way for Socrates, who gathers up the threads anew, and skims the highest points of each of them. But they are not to be regarded as the stages of an idea, rising above one another to a climax. They are fanciful, partly facetious performances, 'yet also having a certain measure of seriousness,' which the successive speakers dedicate to the god. All of them are rhetorical and poetical rather than dialectical, but glimpses of truth appear in them. When Eryximachus says that the principles of music are simple in themselves, but confused in their application, he touches lightly upon a difficulty which has troubled the moderns as well as the ancients in music, and may be extended to the other applied sciences. That confusion begins in the concrete, was the natural feeling of a mind dwelling in the world of ideas. When Pausanias remarks that personal attachments are inimical to despots. The experience of Greek history confirms the truth of his remark. When Aristophanes declares that love is the desire of the whole, he expresses a feeling not unlike that of the German philosopher, who says that 'philosophy is home sickness.' When Agathon says that no man 'can be wronged of his own free will,' he is alluding playfully to a serious problem of Greek philosophy (compare Arist. Nic. Ethics). So naturally does Plato mingle jest and earnest, truth and opinion in the same work.

The characters—of Phaedrus, who has been the cause of more philosophical discussions than any other man, with the exception of Simmias the Theban (Phaedrus); of Aristophanes, who disguises under comic imagery a serious purpose; of Agathon, who in later life is satirized by Aristophanes in the Thesmophoriazusae, for his effeminate manners and the feeble rhythms of his verse; of Alcibiades, who is the same strange contrast of great powers and great vices, which meets us in history—are drawn to the life; and we may suppose the less-known characters of Pausanias and Eryximachus to be also true to the traditional recollection of them (compare Phaedr., Protag.; and compare Sympos. with Phaedr.). We may also remark that Aristodemus is called 'the little' in Xenophon's Memorabilia (compare Symp.).

The speeches have been said to follow each other in pairs: Phaedrus and Pausanias being the ethical, Eryximachus and Aristophanes the physical speakers, while in Agathon and Socrates poetry and philosophy blend together. The speech of Phaedrus is also described as the mythological, that of Pausanias as the political, that of Eryximachus as the scientific, that of Aristophanes as the artistic (!), that of Socrates as the philosophical. But these and similar distinctions are not found in Plato;—they are the points of view of his critics, and seem to impede rather than to assist us in understanding him.

When the turn of Socrates comes round he cannot be allowed to disturb the arrangement made at first. With the leave of Phaedrus he asks a few questions, and then he throws his argument into the form of a speech (compare Gorg., Protag.). But his speech is really the narrative of a dialogue between himself and Diotima. And as at a banquet good manners would not allow him to win a victory either over his host or any of the guests, the superiority which he gains over Agathon is ingeniously represented as having been already gained over himself by her. The artifice has the further advantage of maintaining his accustomed profession of ignorance (compare Menex.). Even his knowledge of the mysteries of love, to which he lays claim here and elsewhere (Lys.), is given by Diotima.

The speeches are attested to us by the very best authority. The madman Apollodorus, who for three years past has made a daily study of the actions of Socrates—to whom the world is summed up in the words 'Great is Socrates'—he has heard them from another 'madman,' Aristodemus, who was the 'shadow' of Socrates in days of old, like him going about barefooted, and who had been present at the time. 'Would you desire better witness?' The extraordinary narrative of Alcibiades is ingeniously represented as admitted by Socrates, whose silence when he is invited to contradict gives consent to the narrator. We may observe, by the way, (1) how the very appearance of Aristodemus by himself is a sufficient indication to Agathon that Socrates has been left behind; also, (2) how the courtesy of Agathon anticipates the excuse which Socrates was to have made on Aristodemus' behalf for coming uninvited; (3) how the story of the fit or trance of Socrates is confirmed by the mention which Alcibiades makes of a similar fit of abstraction occurring when he was serving with the army at Potidaea; like (4) the drinking powers of Socrates and his love of the fair, which receive a similar attestation in the concluding scene; or the attachment of Aristodemus, who is not forgotten when Socrates takes his departure. (5) We may notice the manner in which Socrates himself regards the first five speeches, not as true, but as fanciful and exaggerated encomiums of the god Love; (6) the satirical character of them, shown especially in the appeals to mythology, in the reasons which are given by Zeus for reconstructing the frame of man, or by the Boeotians and Eleans for encouraging male loves; (7) the ruling passion of Socrates for dialectics, who will argue with Agathon instead of making a speech, and will only speak at all upon the condition that he is allowed to speak the truth. We may note also the touch of Socratic irony, (8) which admits of a wide application and reveals a deep insight into the world:—that in speaking of holy things and persons there is a general understanding that you should praise them, not that you should speak the truth about them—this is the sort of praise which Socrates is unable to give. Lastly, (9) we may remark that the banquet is a real banquet after all, at which love is the theme of discourse, and huge quantities of wine are drunk.

The discourse of Phaedrus is half-mythical, half-ethical; and he himself, true to the character which is given him in the Dialogue bearing his name, is half-sophist, half-enthusiast. He is the critic of poetry also, who compares Homer and Aeschylus in the insipid and irrational manner of the schools of the day, characteristically reasoning about the probability of matters which do not admit of reasoning. He starts from a noble text: 'That without the sense of honour and dishonour neither states nor individuals ever do any good or great work.' But he soon passes on to more common-place topics. The antiquity of love, the blessing of having a lover, the incentive which love offers to daring deeds, the examples of Alcestis and Achilles, are the chief themes of his discourse. The love of women is regarded by him as almost on an equality with that of men; and he makes the singular remark that the gods favour the return of love which is made by the beloved more than the original sentiment, because the lover is of a nobler and diviner nature.

There is something of a sophistical ring in the speech of Phaedrus, which recalls the first speech in imitation of Lysias, occurring in the Dialogue called the Phaedrus. This is still more marked in the speech of Pausanias which follows; and which is at once hyperlogical in form and also extremely confused and pedantic. Plato is attacking the logical feebleness of the sophists and rhetoricians, through their pupils, not forgetting by the way to satirize the monotonous and unmeaning rhythms which Prodicus and others were introducing into Attic prose (compare Protag.). Of course, he is 'playing both sides of the game,' as in the Gorgias and Phaedrus; but it is not necessary in order to understand him that we should discuss the fairness of his mode of proceeding. The love of Pausanias for Agathon has already been touched upon in the Protagoras, and is alluded to by Aristophanes. Hence he is naturally the upholder of male loves, which, like all the other affections or actions of men, he regards as varying according to the manner of their performance. Like the sophists and like Plato himself, though in a different sense, he begins his discussion by an appeal to mythology, and distinguishes between the elder and younger love. The value which he attributes to such loves as motives to virtue and philosophy is at variance with modern and Christian notions, but is in accordance with

Hellenic sentiment. The opinion of Christendom has not altogether condemned passionate friendships between persons of the same sex, but has certainly not encouraged them, because though innocent in themselves in a few temperaments they are liable to degenerate into fearful evil. Pausanias is very earnest in the defence of such loves; and he speaks of them as generally approved among Hellenes and disapproved by barbarians. His speech is 'more words than matter,' and might have been composed by a pupil of Lysias or of Prodicus, although there is no hint given that Plato is specially referring to them. As Eryximachus says, 'he makes a fair beginning, but a lame ending.'

Plato transposes the two next speeches, as in the Republic he would transpose the virtues and the mathematical sciences. This is done partly to avoid monotony, partly for the sake of making Aristophanes 'the cause of wit in others,' and also in order to bring the comic and tragic poet into juxtaposition, as if by accident. A suitable 'expectation' of Aristophanes is raised by the ludicrous circumstance of his having the hiccough, which is appropriately cured by his substitute, the physician Eryximachus. To Eryximachus Love is the good physician; he sees everything as an intelligent physicist, and, like many professors of his art in modern times, attempts to reduce the moral to the physical; or recognises one law of love which pervades them both. There are loves and strifes of the body as well as of the mind. Like Hippocrates the Asclepiad, he is a disciple of Heracleitus, whose conception of the harmony of opposites he explains in a new way as the harmony after discord; to his common sense, as to that of many moderns as well as ancients, the identity of contradictories is an absurdity. His notion of love may be summed up as the harmony of man with himself in soul as well as body, and of all things in heaven and earth with one another.

Aristophanes is ready to laugh and make laugh before he opens his mouth, just as Socrates, true to his character, is ready to argue before he begins to speak. He expresses the very genius of the old comedy, its coarse and forcible imagery, and the licence of its language in speaking about the gods. He has no sophistical notions about love, which is brought back by him to its common-sense meaning of love between intelligent beings. His account of the origin of the sexes has the greatest (comic) probability and verisimilitude. Nothing in Aristophanes is more truly Aristophanic than the description of the human monster whirling round on four arms and four legs, eight in all, with incredible rapidity. Yet there is a mixture of earnestness in this jest; three serious principles seem to be insinuated:—first, that man cannot exist in isolation; he must be reunited if he is to be perfected: secondly, that love is the mediator and reconciler of poor, divided human nature: thirdly, that the loves of this world are an indistinct anticipation of an ideal union which is not yet realized.

The speech of Agathon is conceived in a higher strain, and receives the real, if half-ironical, approval of Socrates. It is the speech of the tragic poet and a sort of poem, like tragedy, moving among the gods of Olympus, and not among the elder or Orphic deities. In the idea of the antiquity of love he cannot agree; love is not of the olden time, but present and youthful ever. The speech may be compared with that speech of Socrates in the Phaedrus in which he describes himself as talking dithyrambs. It is at once a preparation for Socrates and a foil to him. The rhetoric of Agathon elevates the soul to 'sunlit heights,' but at the same time contrasts with the natural and necessary eloquence of Socrates. Agathon contributes the distinction between love and the works of love, and also hints incidentally that love is always of beauty, which Socrates afterwards raises into a principle. While the consciousness of discord is stronger in the comic poet Aristophanes, Agathon, the tragic poet, has a deeper sense of harmony and reconciliation, and speaks of Love as the creator and artist.

All the earlier speeches embody common opinions coloured with a tinge of philosophy. They furnish the material out of which Socrates proceeds to form his discourse, starting, as in other places, from mythology and the opinions of men. From Phaedrus he takes the thought that love is stronger than death; from Pausanias, that the true love is akin to intellect and political activity; from Eryximachus, that love is a universal phenomenon and the great power of nature; from Aristophanes, that love is the child of want, and is not merely the love of the congenial or of the whole, but (as he adds) of the good; from Agathon, that love is of beauty, not however of beauty only, but of birth in beauty. As it would be out of character for Socrates to make a lengthened harangue, the speech takes the form of a dialogue between Socrates and a mysterious woman of foreign extraction. She elicits the final truth from one who knows nothing, and who, speaking by the lips of another, and himself a despiser of rhetoric, is proved also to be the most consummate of rhetoricians (compare Menexenus).

The last of the six discourses begins with a short argument which overthrows not only Agathon but all the preceding speakers by the help of a distinction which has escaped them. Extravagant praises have been ascribed to Love as the author of every good; no sort of encomium was too high for him, whether deserved and true or not. But Socrates has no talent for speaking anything but the truth, and if he is to speak the truth of Love he must honestly confess that he is not a good at all: for love is of the good, and no man can desire that which he has. This piece of dialectics is ascribed to Diotima, who has already urged upon Socrates the argument which he urges against Agathon. That the distinction is a fallacy is obvious; it is almost acknowledged to be so by Socrates himself. For he who has beauty or good may desire more of them; and he who has beauty or good in himself may desire beauty and good in others. The fallacy seems to arise out of a confusion between the abstract ideas of good and beauty, which do not admit of degrees, and their partial realization in individuals.

But Diotima, the prophetess of Mantineia, whose sacred and superhuman character raises her above the ordinary proprieties of women, has taught Socrates far more than this about the art and mystery of love. She has taught him that love is another aspect of philosophy. The same want in the human soul which is satisfied in the vulgar by the procreation of children, may become the highest aspiration of intellectual desire. As the Christian might speak of hungering and thirsting after righteousness; or of divine loves under the figure of human (compare Eph. 'This is a great mystery, but I speak concerning Christ and the church'); as the mediaeval saint might speak of the 'fruitio Dei;' as Dante saw all things contained in his love of Beatrice, so Plato would have us absorb all other loves and desires in the love of knowledge. Here is the beginning of Neoplatonism, or rather, perhaps, a proof (of which there are many) that the so-called mysticism of the East was not strange to the Greek of the fifth century before Christ. The first tumult of the affections was not wholly subdued; there were longings of a creature moving about in worlds not realized, which no art could satisfy. To most men reason and passion appear to be antagonistic both in idea and fact. The union of the greatest comprehension of knowledge and the burning intensity of love is a contradiction in nature, which may have existed in a far-off primeval age in the mind of some Hebrew prophet or other Eastern sage, but has now become an imagination only. Yet this 'passion of the reason' is the theme of the Symposium of Plato. And as there is no impossibility in supposing that 'one king, or son of a king, may be a philosopher,' so also there is a probability that there may be some few—perhaps one or two in a whole generation—in whom the light of truth may not lack the warmth of desire. And if there be such natures, no one will be disposed to deny that 'from them flow most of the benefits of individuals and states;' and even from imperfect combinations of the two elements in teachers or statesmen great good may often arise.

Yet there is a higher region in which love is not only felt, but satisfied, in the perfect beauty of eternal knowledge, beginning with the beauty of earthly things, and at last reaching a beauty in which all existence is seen to be harmonious and one. The limited affection is enlarged, and enabled to behold the ideal of all things. And here the highest summit which is reached in the Symposium is seen also to be the highest summit which is attained in the

Republic, but approached from another side; and there is 'a way upwards and downwards,' which is the same and not the same in both. The ideal beauty of the one is the ideal good of the other; regarded not with the eye of knowledge, but of faith and desire; and they are respectively the source of beauty and the source of good in all other things. And by the steps of a 'ladder reaching to heaven' we pass from images of visible beauty (Greek), and from the hypotheses of the Mathematical sciences, which are not yet based upon the idea of good, through the concrete to the abstract, and, by different paths arriving, behold the vision of the eternal (compare Symp. (Greek) Republic (Greek) also Phaedrus). Under one aspect 'the idea is love'; under another, 'truth.' In both the lover of wisdom is the 'spectator of all time and of all existence.' This is a 'mystery' in which Plato also obscurely intimates the union of the spiritual and fleshly, the interpenetration of the moral and intellectual faculties.

The divine image of beauty which resides within Socrates has been revealed; the Silenus, or outward man, has now to be exhibited. The description of Socrates follows immediately after the speech of Socrates; one is the complement of the other. At the height of divine inspiration, when the force of nature can no further go, by way of contrast to this extreme idealism, Alcibiades, accompanied by a troop of revellers and a flute-girl, staggers in, and being drunk is able to tell of things which he would have been ashamed to make known if he had been sober. The state of his affections towards Socrates, unintelligible to us and perverted as they appear, affords an illustration of the power ascribed to the loves of man in the speech of Pausanias. He does not suppose his feelings to be peculiar to himself: there are several other persons in the company who have been equally in love with Socrates, and like himself have been deceived by him. The singular part of this confession is the combination of the most degrading passion with the desire of virtue and improvement. Such an union is not wholly untrue to human nature, which is capable of combining good and evil in a degree beyond what we can easily conceive. In imaginative persons, especially, the God and beast in man seem to part asunder more than is natural in a well-regulated mind. The Platonic Socrates (for of the real Socrates this may be doubted: compare his public rebuke of Critias for his shameful love of Euthydemus in Xenophon, Memorabilia) does not regard the greatest evil of Greek life as a thing not to be spoken of; but it has a ridiculous element (Plato's Symp.), and is a subject for irony, no less than for moral reprobation (compare Plato's Symp.). It is also used as a figure of speech which no one interpreted literally (compare Xen. Symp.). Nor does Plato feel any repugnance, such as would be felt in modern times, at bringing his great master and hero into connexion with nameless crimes. He is contented with representing him as a saint, who has won 'the Olympian victory' over the temptations of human nature. The fault of taste, which to us is so glaring and which was recognized by the Greeks of a later age (Athenaeus), was not perceived by Plato himself. We are still more surprised to find that the philosopher is incited to take the first step in his upward progress (Symp.) by the beauty of young men and boys, which was alone capable of inspiring the modern feeling of romance in the Greek mind. The passion of love took the spurious form of an enthusiasm for the ideal of beauty—a worship as of some godlike image of an Apollo or Antinous. But the love of youth when not depraved was a love of virtue and modesty as well as of beauty, the one being the expression of the other; and in certain Greek states, especially at Sparta and Thebes, the honourable attachment of a youth to an elder man was a part of his education. The 'army of lovers and their beloved who would be invincible if they could be united by such a tie' (Symp.), is not a mere fiction of Plato's, but seems actually to have existed at Thebes in the days of Epaminondas and Pelopidas, if we may believe writers cited anonymously by Plutarch, Pelop. Vit. It is observable that Plato never in the least degree excuses the depraved love of the body (compare Charm.; Rep.; Laws; Symp.; and once more Xenophon, Mem.), nor is there any Greek writer of mark who condones or approves such connexions. But owing partly to the puzzling nature of the subject these friendships are spoken of by Plato in a manner different from that customary among ourselves. To most of them we should hesitate to ascribe, any more than to the attachment of Achilles and Patroclus in Homer, an immoral or licentious character. There were many, doubtless, to whom the love of the fair mind was the noblest form of friendship (Rep.), and who deemed the friendship of man with man to be higher than the love of woman, because altogether separated from the bodily appetites. The existence of such attachments may be reasonably attributed to the inferiority and seclusion of woman, and the want of a real family or social life and parental influence in Hellenic cities; and they were encouraged by the practice of gymnastic exercises, by the meetings of political clubs, and by the tie of military companionship. They were also an educational institution: a young person was specially entrusted by his parents to some elder friend who was expected by them to train their son in manly exercises and in virtue. It is not likely that a Greek parent committed him to a lover, any more than we should to a schoolmaster, in the expectation that he would be corrupted by him, but rather in the hope that his morals would be better cared for than was possible in a great household of slaves.

It is difficult to adduce the authority of Plato either for or against such practices or customs, because it is not always easy to determine whether he is speaking of 'the heavenly and philosophical love, or of the coarse Polyhymnia:' and he often refers to this (e.g. in the Symposium) half in jest, yet 'with a certain degree of seriousness.' We observe that they entered into one part of Greek literature, but not into another, and that the larger part is free from such associations. Indecency was an element of the ludicrous in the old Greek Comedy, as it has been in other ages and countries. But effeminate love was always condemned as well as ridiculed by the Comic poets; and in the New Comedy the allusions to such topics have disappeared. They seem to have been no longer tolerated by the greater refinement of the age. False sentiment is found in the Lyric and Elegiac poets; and in mythology 'the greatest of the Gods' (Rep.) is not exempt from evil imputations. But the morals of a nation are not to be judged of wholly by its literature. Hellas was not necessarily more corrupted in the days of the Persian and Peloponnesian wars, or of Plato and the Orators, than England in the time of Fielding and Smollett, or France in the nineteenth century. No one supposes certain French novels to be a representation of ordinary French life. And the greater part of Greek literature, beginning with Homer and including the tragedians, philosophers, and, with the exception of the Comic poets (whose business was to raise a laugh by whatever means), all the greater writers of Hellas who have been preserved to us, are free from the taint of indecency.

Some general considerations occur to our mind when we begin to reflect on this subject. (1) That good and evil are linked together in human nature, and have often existed side by side in the world and in man to an extent hardly credible. We cannot distinguish them, and are therefore unable to part them; as in the parable 'they grow together unto the harvest:' it is only a rule of external decency by which society can divide them. Nor should we be right in inferring from the prevalence of any one vice or corruption that a state or individual was demoralized in their whole character. Not only has the corruption of the best been sometimes thought to be the worst, but it may be remarked that this very excess of evil has been the stimulus to good (compare Plato, Laws, where he says that in the most corrupt cities individuals are to be found beyond all praise). (2) It may be observed that evils which admit of degrees can seldom be rightly estimated, because under the same name actions of the most different degrees of culpability may be included. No charge is more easily set going than the imputation of secret wickedness (which cannot be either proved or disproved and often cannot be defined) when directed against a person of whom the world, or a section of it, is predisposed to think evil. And it is quite possible that the malignity of Greek scandal, aroused by some personal jealousy or party enmity, may have converted the innocent friendship of a great man for a noble youth into a connexion of another kind. Such accusations were brought against several of the leading men of Hellas, e.g. Cimon, Alcibiades, Critias, Demosthenes, Epaminondas: several of the Roman emperors were assailed by similar weapons which have been used even in our own day against statesmen of the highest character. (3) While we know that in this matter there is a great gulf fixed between Greek and Christian Ethics, yet, if we would do justice to the Greeks, we must also acknowledge that there was a greater outspokenness among them than among ourselves about the things which nature hides, and that the more frequent mention of such topics is not to be taken as the measure of the prevalence of offences, or as a proof of the general corruption of society. It is likely that every religion in the world has used words or practised rites in one age, which have become distasteful or repugnant to another. We cannot, though for different reasons, trust the representations either of Comedy or Satire; and still less of Christian Apologists. (4) We observe that at Thebes and Lacedemon the attachment of an elder friend to a beloved youth was often deemed to be a part of his education; and was encouraged by his parents—it was only shameful if it degenerated into licentiousness. Such we may believe to have been the tie which united Asophychus and Cephisodorus with the great Epaminondas in whose companionship they fell (Plutarch, Amat.; Athenaeus on the authority of Theopompus). (5) A small matter: there appears to be a difference of custom among the Greeks and among ourselves, as between ourselves and continental nations at the present time, in modes of salutation. We must not suspect evil in the hearty kiss or embrace of a male friend 'returning from the army at Potidaea' any more than in a similar salutation when practised by members of the same family. But those who make these admissions, and who regard, not without pity, the victims of such illusions in our own day, whose life has been blasted by them, may be none the less resolved that the natural and healthy instincts of mankind shall alone be tolerated (Greek); and that the lesson of manliness which we have inherited from our fathers shall not degenerate into sentimentalism or effeminacy. The possibility of an honourable connexion of this kind seems to have died out with Greek civilization. Among the Romans, and also among barbarians, such as the Celts and Persians, there is no trace of such attachments existing in any noble or virtuous form.

(Compare Hoeck's Creta and the admirable and exhaustive article of Meier in Ersch and Grueber's Cyclopedia on this subject; Plutarch, Amatores; Athenaeus; Lysias contra Simonem; Aesch. c. Timarchum.)

The character of Alcibiades in the Symposium is hardly less remarkable than that of Socrates, and agrees with the picture given of him in the first of the two Dialogues which are called by his name, and also with the slight sketch of him in the Protagoras. He is the impersonation of lawlessness—'the lion's whelp, who ought not to be reared in the city,' yet not without a certain generosity which gained the hearts of men,—strangely fascinated by Socrates, and possessed of a genius which might have been either the destruction or salvation of Athens. The dramatic interest of the character is heightened by the recollection of his after history. He seems to have been present to the mind of Plato in the description of the democratic man of the Republic (compare also Alcibiades 1).

There is no criterion of the date of the Symposium, except that which is furnished by the allusion to the division of Arcadia after the destruction of Mantinea. This took place in the year B.C. 384, which is the forty-fourth year of Plato's life. The Symposium cannot therefore be regarded as a youthful work. As Mantinea was restored in the year 369, the composition of the Dialogue will probably fall between 384 and 369. Whether the recollection of the event is more likely to have been renewed at the destruction or restoration of the city, rather than at some intermediate period, is a consideration not worth raising.

The Symposium is connected with the Phaedrus both in style and subject; they are the only Dialogues of Plato in which the theme of love is discussed at length. In both of them philosophy is regarded as a sort of enthusiasm or madness; Socrates is himself 'a prophet new inspired' with Bacchanalian revelry, which, like his philosophy, he characteristically pretends to have derived not from himself but from others. The Phaedo also presents some points of comparison with the Symposium. For there, too, philosophy might be described as 'dying for love;' and there are not wanting many touches of humour and fancy, which remind us of the Symposium. But while the Phaedo and Phaedrus look backwards and forwards to past and future states of existence, in the Symposium there is no break between this world and another; and we rise from one to the other by a regular series of steps or stages, proceeding from the particulars of sense to the universal of reason, and from one universal to many, which are finally reunited in a single science (compare Rep.). At first immortality means only the succession of existences; even knowledge comes and goes. Then follows, in the language of the mysteries, a higher and a higher degree of initiation; at last we arrive at the perfect vision of beauty, not relative or changing, but eternal and absolute; not bounded by this world, or in or out of this world, but an aspect of the divine, extending over all things, and having no limit of space or time: this is the highest knowledge of which the human mind is capable. Plato does not go on to ask whether the individual is absorbed in the sea of light and beauty or retains his personality. Enough for him to have attained the true beauty or good, without enquiring precisely into the relation in which human beings stood to it. That the soul has such a reach of thought, and is capable of partaking of the eternal nature, seems to imply that she too is eternal (compare Phaedrus). But Plato does not distinguish the eternal in man from the eternal in the world or in God. He is willing to rest in the contemplation of the idea, which to him is the cause of all things (Rep.), and has no strength to go further.

The Symposium of Xenophon, in which Socrates describes himself as a pander, and also discourses of the difference between sensual and sentimental love, likewise offers several interesting points of comparison. But the suspicion which hangs over other writings of Xenophon, and the numerous minute references to the Phaedrus and Symposium, as well as to some of the other writings of Plato, throw a doubt on the genuineness of the work. The Symposium of Xenophon, if written by him at all, would certainly show that he wrote against Plato, and was acquainted with his works. Of this hostility there is no trace in the Memorabilia. Such a rivalry is more characteristic of an imitator than of an original writer. The (so-called) Symposium of Xenophon may therefore have no more title to be regarded as genuine than the confessedly spurious Apology.

There are no means of determining the relative order in time of the Phaedrus, Symposium, Phaedo. The order which has been adopted in this translation rests on no other principle than the desire to bring together in a series the memorials of the life of Socrates.

SYMPOSIUM

PERSONS OF THE DIALOGUE: Apollodorus, who repeats to his companion the dialogue which he had heard from Aristodemus, and had already once narrated to Glaucon. Phaedrus, Pausanias, Eryximachus, Aristophanes, Agathon, Socrates, Alcibiades, A Troop of Revellers.
SCENE: The House of Agathon.

Concerning the things about which you ask to be informed I believe that I am not ill-prepared with an answer. For the day before yesterday I was coming from my own home at Phalerum to the city, and one of my acquaintance, who had caught a sight of me from behind, calling out playfully in the distance, said: Apollodorus, O thou Phalerian (Probably a play of words on (Greek), 'bald-headed.') man, halt! So I did as I was bid; and then he said, I was looking for you, Apollodorus, only just now, that I might ask you about the speeches in praise of love, which were delivered by Socrates, Alcibiades, and others, at Agathon's supper. Phoenix, the son of Philip, told another person who told me of them; his narrative was very indistinct, but he said that you knew, and I wish that you would give me an account of them. Who, if not you, should be the reporter of the words of your friend? And first tell me, he said, were you present at this meeting?

Your informant, Glaucon, I said, must have been very indistinct indeed, if you imagine that the occasion was recent; or that I could have been of the party.

Why, yes, he replied, I thought so.

Impossible: I said. Are you ignorant that for many years Agathon has not resided at Athens; and not three have elapsed since I became acquainted with Socrates, and have made it my daily business to know all that he says and does. There was a time when I was running about the world, fancying myself to be well employed, but I was really a most wretched being, no better than you are now. I thought that I ought to do anything rather than be a philosopher.

Well, he said, jesting apart, tell me when the meeting occurred.

In our boyhood, I replied, when Agathon won the prize with his first tragedy, on the day after that on which he and his chorus offered the sacrifice of victory.

Then it must have been a long while ago, he said; and who told you—did Socrates?

No indeed, I replied, but the same person who told Phoenix;—he was a little fellow, who never wore any shoes, Aristodemus, of the deme of Cydathenaeum. He had been at Agathon's feast; and I think that in those days there was no one who was a more devoted admirer of Socrates. Moreover, I have asked Socrates about the truth of some parts of his narrative, and he confirmed them.

Then, said Glaucon, let us have the tale over again; is not the road to Athens just made for conversation? And so we walked, and talked of the discourses on love; and therefore, as I said at first, I am not ill-prepared to comply with your request, and will have another rehearsal of them if you like. For to speak or to hear others speak of philosophy always gives me the greatest pleasure, to say nothing of the profit. But when I hear another strain, especially that of you rich men and traders, such conversation displeases me; and I pity you who are my companions, because you think that you are doing something when in reality you are doing nothing. And I dare say that you pity me in return, whom you regard as an unhappy creature, and very probably you are right. But I certainly know of you what you only think of me—there is the difference.

COMPANION: I see, Apollodorus, that you are just the same—always speaking evil of yourself, and of others; and I do believe that you pity all mankind, with the exception of Socrates, yourself first of all, true in this to your old name, which, however deserved, I know not how you acquired, of Apollodorus the madman; for you are always raging against yourself and everybody but Socrates.

APOLLODORUS: Yes, friend, and the reason why I am said to be mad, and out of my wits, is just because I have these notions of myself and you; no other evidence is required.

COMPANION: No more of that, Apollodorus; but let me renew my request that you would repeat the conversation.

APOLLODORUS: Well, the tale of love was on this

3

wise:—But perhaps I had better begin at the beginning, and endeavour to give you the exact words of Aristodemus:

He said that he met Socrates fresh from the bath and sandalled; and as the sight of the sandals was unusual, he asked him whither he was going that he had been converted into such a beau:—

To a banquet at Agathon's, he replied, whose invitation to his sacrifice of victory I refused yesterday, fearing a crowd, but promising that I would come to-day instead; and so I have put on my finery, because he is such a fine man. What say you to going with me unasked?

I will do as you bid me, I replied.

Follow then, he said, and let us demolish the proverb:—

'To the feasts of inferior men the good unbidden go;'

instead of which our proverb will run:—

'To the feasts of the good the good unbidden go;'

and this alteration may be supported by the authority of Homer himself, who not only demolishes but literally outrages the proverb. For, after picturing Agamemnon as the most valiant of men, he makes Menelaus, who is but a fainthearted warrior, come unbidden (Iliad) to the banquet of Agamemnon, who is feasting and offering sacrifices, not the better to the worse, but the worse to the better.

I rather fear, Socrates, said Aristodemus, lest this may still be my case; and that, like Menelaus in Homer, I shall be the inferior person, who

'To the feasts of the wise unbidden goes.'

But I shall say that I was bidden of you, and then you will have to make an excuse.

'Two going together,'

4

he replied, in Homeric fashion, one or other of them may invent an excuse by the way (Iliad).

This was the style of their conversation as they went along. Socrates dropped behind in a fit of abstraction, and desired Aristodemus, who was waiting, to go on before him. When he reached the house of Agathon he found the doors wide open, and a comical thing happened. A servant coming out met him, and led him at once into the banqueting-hall in which the guests were reclining, for the banquet was about to begin. Welcome, Aristodemus, said Agathon, as soon as he appeared—you are just in time to sup with us; if you come on any other matter put it off, and make one of us, as I was looking for you yesterday and meant to have asked you, if I could have found you. But what have you done with Socrates?

I turned round, but Socrates was nowhere to be seen; and I had to explain that he had been with me a moment before, and that I came by his invitation to the supper.

You were quite right in coming, said Agathon; but where is he himself?

He was behind me just now, as I entered, he said, and I cannot think what has become of him.

Go and look for him, boy, said Agathon, and bring him in; and do you, Aristodemus, meanwhile take the place by Eryximachus.

The servant then assisted him to wash, and he lay down, and presently another servant came in and reported that our friend Socrates had retired into the portico of the neighbouring house. 'There he is fixed,' said he, 'and when I call to him he will not stir.'

How strange, said Agathon; then you must call him again, and keep calling him.

Let him alone, said my informant; he has a way of stopping anywhere and losing himself without any reason. I believe that he will soon appear; do not therefore disturb him.

Well, if you think so, I will leave him, said Agathon. And then, turning to the servants, he added, 'Let us have supper without waiting for him. Serve up whatever you please, for there is no one to give you orders; hitherto I have never left you to yourselves. But on this occasion imagine that you are our hosts, and that I and the company are your guests; treat us well, and then we shall commend you.' After this, supper was served, but still no Socrates; and during the meal Agathon several times expressed a wish to send for him, but Aristodemus objected; and at last when the feast was about half over—for the fit, as usual, was not of long duration— Socrates entered. Agathon, who was reclining alone at the end of the table, begged that he would take the place next to him; that 'I may touch you,' he said, 'and have the benefit of that wise thought which came into your mind in the portico, and is now in your possession; for I am certain that you would not have come away until you had found what you sought.'

How I wish, said Socrates, taking his place as he was desired, that wisdom could be infused by touch, out of the fuller into the emptier man, as water runs through wool out of a fuller cup into an emptier one; if that were so, how greatly should I value the privilege of reclining at your side! For you would have filled me full with a stream of wisdom plenteous and fair; whereas my own is of a very mean and questionable sort, no better than a dream. But yours is bright and full of promise, and was manifested forth in all the splendour of youth the day before yesterday, in the presence of more than thirty thousand Hellenes.

You are mocking, Socrates, said Agathon, and ere long you and I will have to determine who bears off the palm of wisdom—of this Dionysus shall be the judge; but at present you are better occupied with supper.

Socrates took his place on the couch, and supped with the rest; and then libations were offered, and after a hymn had been sung to the god, and there had been the usual ceremonies, they were about to commence drinking, when Pausanias said, And now, my friends, how can we drink with least injury to ourselves? I can assure you that I feel severely the effect of yesterday's potations, and must have time to recover; and I suspect that most of you are in the same predicament, for you were of the party yesterday. Consider then: How can the drinking be made easiest?

I entirely agree, said Aristophanes, that we should, by all means, avoid hard drinking, for I was myself one of those who were yesterday drowned in drink.

I think that you are right, said Eryximachus, the son of Acumenus; but I should still like to hear one other person speak: Is Agathon able to drink hard?

I am not equal to it, said Agathon.

Then, said Eryximachus, the weak heads like myself, Aristodemus, Phaedrus, and others who never can drink, are fortunate in finding that the stronger ones are not in a drinking mood. (I do not include Socrates, who is able either to drink or to abstain, and will not mind, whichever we do.) Well, as of none of the company seem disposed to drink much, I may be forgiven for saying, as a physician, that drinking deep is a bad practice, which I never follow, if I can help, and certainly do not recommend to another, least of all to any one who still feels the effects of yesterday's carouse.

I always do what you advise, and especially what you prescribe as a physician, rejoined Phaedrus the Myrrhinusian, and the rest of the company, if they are wise, will do the same.

It was agreed that drinking was not to be the order of the day, but that they were all to drink only so much as they pleased.

Then, said Eryximachus, as you are all agreed that drinking is to be voluntary, and that there is to be no compulsion, I move, in the next place, that the flute-girl, who has just made her appearance, be told to go away and play to herself, or, if she likes, to the women who are within (compare Prot.). To-day let us have conversation instead; and, if you will allow me, I will tell you what sort of conversation. This proposal having been accepted, Eryximachus proceeded as follows:—

I will begin, he said, after the manner of Melanippe in Euripides,

'Not mine the word'

which I am about to speak, but that of Phaedrus. For often he says to me in an indignant tone:—'What a strange thing it is, Eryximachus, that, whereas other gods have poems and hymns made in their honour, the great and glorious god, Love, has no encomiast among all the poets who are so many. There are the worthy sophists too—the excellent Prodicus for example, who have descanted in prose on the virtues of Heracles and other heroes; and, what is still more extraordinary, I have met with a philosophical work in which the utility of salt has been made the theme of an eloquent discourse; and many other like things have had a like honour bestowed upon them. And only to think that there should have been an eager interest created about them, and yet that to this day no one has ever dared worthily to hymn Love's praises! So entirely has this great deity been neglected.' Now in this Phaedrus seems to me to be quite right, and therefore I want to offer him a contribution; also I think that at the present moment we who are here assembled cannot do better than honour the god Love. If you agree with me, there will be no lack of conversation; for I mean to propose that each of us in turn, going from left to right, shall make a speech in honour of Love. Let him give us the best which he can; and Phaedrus, because he is sitting first on the left hand, and because he is the father of the thought, shall begin.

No one will vote against you, Eryximachus, said Socrates. How can I oppose your motion, who profess to understand nothing but matters of love; nor, I presume, will Agathon and Pausanias; and there can be no doubt of Aristophanes, whose whole concern is with Dionysus and Aphrodite; nor will any one disagree of those whom I see around me. The proposal, as I am aware, may seem rather hard upon us whose place is last; but we shall be contented if we hear some good speeches first. Let Phaedrus begin the praise of Love, and good luck to him. All the company expressed their assent, and desired him to do as Socrates bade him.

Aristodemus did not recollect all that was said, nor do I

recollect all that he related to me; but I will tell you what I thought most worthy of remembrance, and what the chief speakers said.

Phaedrus began by affirming that Love is a mighty god, and wonderful among gods and men, but especially wonderful in his birth. For he is the eldest of the gods, which is an honour to him; and a proof of his claim to this honour is, that of his parents there is no memorial; neither poet nor prose-writer has ever affirmed that he had any. As Hesiod says:—

'First Chaos came, and then broad-bosomed Earth, The everlasting seat of all that is, And Love.'

In other words, after Chaos, the Earth and Love, these two, came into being. Also Parmenides sings of Generation:

'First in the train of gods, he fashioned Love.'

And Acusilaus agrees with Hesiod. Thus numerous are the witnesses who acknowledge Love to be the eldest of the gods. And not only is he the eldest, he is also the source of the greatest benefits to us. For I know not any greater blessing to a young man who is beginning life than a virtuous lover, or to the lover than a beloved youth. For the principle which ought to be the guide of men who would nobly live—that principle, I say, neither kindred, nor honour, nor wealth, nor any other motive is able to implant so well as love. Of what am I speaking? Of the sense of honour and dishonour, without which neither states nor individuals ever do any good or great work. And I say that a lover who is detected in doing any dishonourable act, or submitting through cowardice when any dishonour is done to him by another, will be more pained at being detected by his beloved than at being seen by his father, or by his companions, or by any one else. The beloved too, when he is found in any disgraceful situation, has the same feeling about his lover. And if there were only some way of contriving that a state or an army should be made up of lovers and their loves (compare Rep.), they would be the very best governors of their own city, abstaining from all dishonour, and emulating one another in honour; and when fighting at each other's side, although a mere handful, they would overcome the world. For what lover would not choose rather to be seen by all mankind than by his beloved, either when abandoning his post or throwing away his arms? He would be ready to die a thousand deaths rather than endure this. Or who would desert his beloved or fail him in the hour of danger? The veriest coward would become an inspired hero, equal to the bravest, at such a time; Love would inspire him. That courage which, as Homer says, the god breathes into the souls of some heroes, Love of his own nature infuses into the lover.

Love will make men dare to die for their beloved—love alone; and women as well as men. Of this, Alcestis, the daughter of Pelias, is a monument to all Hellas; for she was willing to lay down her life on behalf of her husband, when no one else would, although he had a father and mother; but the tenderness of her love so far exceeded theirs, that she made them seem to be strangers in blood to their own son, and in name only related to him; and so noble did this action of hers appear to the gods, as well as to men, that among the many who have done virtuously she is one of the very few to whom, in admiration of her noble action, they have granted the privilege of returning alive to earth; such exceeding honour is paid by the gods to the devotion and virtue of love. But Orpheus, the son of Oeagrus, the harper, they sent empty away, and presented to him an apparition only of her whom he sought, but herself they would not give up, because he showed no spirit; he was only a harp-player, and did not dare like Alcestis to die for love, but was contriving how he might enter Hades alive; moreover, they afterwards caused him to suffer death at the hands of women, as the punishment of his cowardliness. Very different was the reward of the true love of Achilles towards his lover Patroclus—his lover and not his love (the notion that Patroclus was the beloved one is a foolish error into which Aeschylus has fallen, for Achilles was surely the fairer of the two, fairer also than all the other heroes; and, as Homer informs us, he was still beardless, and younger far). And greatly as the gods honour the virtue of love, still the return of love on the part of the beloved to the lover is more admired and valued and rewarded by them, for the lover is more divine; because he is inspired by God. Now Achilles was quite aware, for he had been told by his mother, that he might avoid death and return home, and live to a good old age, if he abstained from slaying Hector. Nevertheless he gave his life to revenge his friend, and dared to die, not only in his defence, but after he was dead. Wherefore the gods honoured him even above Alcestis, and sent him to the Islands of the Blest. These are my reasons for affirming that Love is the eldest and noblest and mightiest of the gods; and the chiefest author and giver of virtue in life, and of happiness after death.

This, or something like this, was the speech of Phaedrus; and some other speeches followed which Aristodemus did not remember; the next which he repeated was that of

Pausanias. Phaedrus, he said, the argument has not been set before us, I think, quite in the right form;—we should not be called upon to praise Love in such an indiscriminate manner. If there were only one Love, then what you said would be well enough; but since there are more Loves than one,—should have begun by determining which of them was to be the theme of our praises. I will amend this defect; and first of all I will tell you which Love is deserving of praise, and then try to hymn the praiseworthy one in a manner worthy of him. For we all know that Love is inseparable from Aphrodite, and if there were only one Aphrodite there would be only one Love; but as there are two goddesses there must be two Loves. And am I not right in asserting that there are two goddesses? The elder one, having no mother, who is called the heavenly Aphrodite— she is the daughter of Uranus; the younger, who is the daughter of Zeus and Dione—her we call common; and the Love who is her fellow-worker is rightly named common, as the other love is called heavenly. All the gods ought to have praise given to them, but not without distinction of their natures; and therefore I must try to distinguish the characters of the two Loves. Now actions vary according to the manner of their performance. Take, for example, that which we are now doing, drinking, singing and talking— these actions are not in themselves either good or evil, but they turn out in this or that way according to the mode of performing them; and when well done they are good, and when wrongly done they are evil; and in like manner not every love, but only that which has a noble purpose, is noble and worthy of praise. The Love who is the offspring of the common Aphrodite is essentially common, and has no discrimination, being such as the meaner sort of men feel, and is apt to be of women as well as of youths, and is of the body rather than of the soul—the most foolish beings are the objects of this love which desires only to gain an end, but never thinks of accomplishing the end nobly, and therefore does good and evil quite indiscriminately. The goddess who is his mother is far younger than the other, and she was born of the union of the male and female, and partakes of both. But the offspring of the heavenly Aphrodite is derived from a mother in whose birth the female has no part,—she is from the male only; this is that love which is of youths, and the goddess being older, there is nothing of wantonness in her. Those who are inspired by this love turn to the male, and delight in him who is the more valiant and intelligent nature; any one may recognise the pure enthusiasts in the very character of their attachments. For they love not boys, but intelligent beings whose reason is beginning to be developed, much about the time at which their beards begin to grow. And in choosing young men to be their companions, they mean to be faithful to them, and pass their whole life in company with them, not to take them in their inexperience, and deceive them, and play the fool with them, or run away from one to another of them. But the love of young boys should be forbidden by law, because their future is uncertain; they may turn out good or bad, either in body or soul, and much noble enthusiasm may be thrown away upon them; in this matter the good are a law to themselves, and the coarser sort of lovers ought to be restrained by force; as we restrain or attempt to restrain them from fixing their affections on women of free birth. These are the persons who bring a reproach on love; and some have been led to deny the lawfulness of such attachments because they see the impropriety and evil of them; for surely nothing that is decorously and lawfully done can justly be censured. Now here and in Lacedaemon the rules about love are perplexing, but in most cities they are simple and easily intelligible; in Elis and Boeotia, and in countries having no gifts of eloquence, they are very straightforward; the law is simply in favour of these connexions, and no one, whether young or old, has anything to say to their discredit; the reason being, as I suppose, that they are men of few words in those parts, and therefore the lovers do not like the trouble of pleading their suit. In Ionia and other places, and generally in countries which are subject to the barbarians, the custom is held to be dishonourable; loves of youths share the evil repute in which philosophy and gymnastics are held, because they are inimical to tyranny; for the interests of rulers require that their subjects should be poor in spirit (compare Arist. Politics), and that there should be no strong bond of friendship or society among them, which love, above all other motives, is likely to inspire, as our Athenian tyrants learned by experience; for the love of Aristogeiton and the constancy of Harmodius had a strength which undid their power. And, therefore, the ill-repute into which these attachments have fallen is to be ascribed to the evil condition of those who make them to be ill-reputed; that is to say, to the self-seeking of the governors and the cowardice of the governed; on the other hand, the indiscriminate honour which is given to them in some countries is attributable to the laziness of those who hold this opinion of them. In our own country a far better principle prevails, but, as I was saying, the explanation of it is rather perplexing. For, observe that open loves are held to be more honourable than secret ones, and that the love of the noblest and highest, even if their persons are less beautiful than others, is especially honourable. Consider, too, how great is the encouragement which all the world gives to the lover; neither is he supposed to be doing anything dishonourable; but if he succeeds he is praised, and if he fail he is blamed. And in the pursuit of his love the custom of mankind allows him to do many strange things, which philosophy would bitterly censure if they were done from any motive of interest, or wish for office or power. He may pray, and entreat, and supplicate, and swear, and lie on a mat at the door, and endure a slavery worse than that of any slave—in any other case friends and enemies would be equally ready to prevent him, but now there is no friend who will be ashamed of him and admonish him, and no enemy will charge him with meanness or flattery; the actions of a lover have a grace which ennobles them; and custom has decided that they are highly commendable and that there no loss of character in them; and, what is strangest of all, he only may swear and forswear himself (so men say), and the gods will forgive his transgression, for there is no such thing as a lover's oath. Such is the entire liberty which gods and men have allowed the lover, according to the custom which prevails in our part of the world. From this point of view a man fairly argues that in Athens to love and to be loved is held to be a very honourable thing. But when parents forbid their sons to talk with their lovers, and place them under a tutor's care, who is appointed to see to these things, and their companions and equals cast in their teeth anything of the sort which they may observe, and their elders refuse to silence the reprovers and do not rebuke them—any one who reflects on all this will, on the contrary, think that we hold these practices to be most disgraceful. But, as I was saying at first, the truth as I imagine is, that whether such practices are honourable or whether they are dishonourable is not a simple question; they are honourable to him who follows them honourably, dishonourable to him who follows them dishonourably. There is dishonour in yielding to the evil, or in an evil manner; but there is honour in yielding to the good, or in an honourable manner. Evil is the vulgar lover who loves the body rather than the soul, inasmuch as he is not even stable, because he loves a thing which is in itself unstable, and therefore when the bloom of youth which he was desiring is over, he takes wing and flies away, in spite of all his words and promises; whereas the love of the noble disposition is life-long, for it becomes one with the everlasting. The custom of our country would have both of them proven well and truly, and would have us yield to the one sort of lover and avoid the other, and therefore encourages some to pursue, and others to fly; testing both the lover and beloved in contests and trials, until they show to which of the two classes they respectively belong. And this is the reason why, in the first place, a hasty attachment is held to be dishonourable, because time is the true test of this as of most other things; and secondly there is a dishonour in being overcome by the love of money, or of wealth, or of political power, whether a man is frightened into surrender by the loss of them, or, having experienced the benefits of money and political corruption, is unable to rise above the seductions of them. For none of these things are of a permanent or lasting nature; not to mention that no generous friendship ever sprang from them. There remains, then, only one way of honourable attachment which custom allows in the beloved, and this is the way of virtue; for as we admitted that any service which the lover does to him is not to be accounted flattery or a dishonour to himself, so the beloved has one way only of voluntary service which is not dishonourable, and this is virtuous service.

For we have a custom, and according to our custom any one who does service to another under the idea that he will be improved by him either in wisdom, or in some other particular of virtue—such a voluntary service, I say, is not to be regarded as a dishonour, and is not open to the charge of flattery. And these two customs, one the love of youth, and the other the practice of philosophy and virtue in general, ought to meet in one, and then the beloved may honourably indulge the lover. For when the lover and beloved come together, having each of them a law, and the lover thinks that he is right in doing any service which he can to his gracious loving one; and the other that he is right in showing any kindness which he can to him who is making him wise and good; the one capable of communicating wisdom and virtue, the other seeking to acquire them with a view to education and wisdom, when the two laws of love are fulfilled and meet in one—then, and then only, may the beloved yield with honour to the lover. Nor when love is of this disinterested sort is there any disgrace in being deceived, but in every other case there is equal disgrace in being or not being deceived. For he who is gracious to his lover under the impression that he is rich, and is disappointed of his gains because he turns out to be poor, is disgraced all the same: for he has done his best to show that he would give himself up to any one's 'uses base' for the sake of money; but this is not honourable. And on the same principle he who gives himself to a lover because he is a good man, and in the hope that he will be improved by his company, shows himself to be virtuous, even though the object of his affection turn out to be a villain, and to have no virtue; and if he is deceived he has committed a noble error. For he has proved that for his part he will do anything for anybody with a view to virtue and improvement, than which there can be nothing nobler. Thus noble in every case is the acceptance of another for the sake of virtue. This is that love which is the love of the heavenly godess, and is heavenly, and of great price to individuals and cities, making the lover and the beloved alike eager in the work of their own improvement. But all other loves are the offspring of the other, who is the common goddess. To you, Phaedrus, I offer this my contribution in praise of love, which is as good as I could make extempore.

Pausanias came to a pause—this is the balanced way in which I have been taught by the wise to speak; and Aristodemus said that the turn of Aristophanes was next, but either he had eaten too much, or from some other cause he had the hiccough, and was obliged to change turns with Eryximachus the physician, who was reclining on the couch below him. Eryximachus, he said, you ought either to stop my hiccough, or to speak in my turn until I have left off.

I will do both, said Eryximachus: I will speak in your turn, and do you speak in mine; and while I am speaking let me recommend you to hold your breath, and if after you have done so for some time the hiccough is no better, then gargle with a little water; and if it still continues, tickle your nose with something and sneeze; and if you sneeze once or twice, even the most violent hiccough is sure to go. I will do as you prescribe, said Aristophanes, and now get on.

Eryximachus spoke as follows: Seeing that Pausanias made a fair beginning, and but a lame ending, I must endeavour to supply his deficiency. I think that he has rightly distinguished two kinds of love. But my art further informs me that the double love is not merely an affection of the soul of man towards the fair, or towards anything, but is to be found in the bodies of all animals and in productions of the earth, and I may say in all that is; such is the conclusion which I seem to have gathered from my own art of medicine, whence I learn how great and wonderful and universal is the deity of love, whose empire extends over all things, divine as well as human. And from medicine I will begin that I may do honour to my art. There are in the human body these two kinds of love, which are confessedly different and unlike, and being unlike, they have loves and desires which are unlike; and the desire of the healthy is one, and the desire of the diseased is another; and as Pausanias was just now saying that to indulge good men is honourable, and bad men dishonourable:—so too in the body the good and healthy elements are to be indulged, and the bad elements and the elements of disease are not to be indulged, but discouraged. And this is what the physician has to do, and in this the art of medicine consists: for medicine may be regarded generally as the knowledge of the loves and desires of the body, and how to satisfy them or not; and the best physician is he who is able to separate fair love from foul, or to convert one into the other; and he who knows how to eradicate and how to implant love, whichever is required, and can reconcile the most hostile elements in the constitution and make them loving friends, is a skilful practitioner. Now the most hostile are the most opposite, such as hot and cold, bitter and sweet, moist and dry, and the like. And my ancestor, Asclepius, knowing how to implant friendship and accord in these elements, was the creator of our art, as our friends the poets here tell us, and I believe them; and not only medicine in every branch but the arts of gymnastic and husbandry are under his dominion. Any one who pays the least attention to the subject will also perceive that in music there is the same reconciliation of opposites; and I suppose that this must have been the meaning of Heracleitus, although his words are not accurate; for he says that The One is united by disunion, like the harmony of the bow and the lyre. Now there is an absurdity saying that harmony is discord or is composed of elements which are still in a state of discord. But what he probably meant was, that harmony is composed of differing notes of higher or lower pitch which disagreed once, but are now reconciled by the art of music; for if the higher and lower notes still disagreed, there could be no harmony,— clearly not. For harmony is a symphony, and symphony is an agreement; but an agreement of disagreements while they disagree there cannot be; you cannot harmonize that which disagrees. In like manner rhythm is compounded of elements short and long, once differing and now in accord; which accordance, as in the former instance, medicine, so in all these other cases, music implants, making love and unison to grow up among them; and thus music, too, is concerned with the principles of love in their application to harmony and rhythm. Again, in the essential nature of harmony and rhythm there is no difficulty in discerning love which has not yet become double. But when you want to use them in actual life, either in the composition of songs or in the correct performance of airs or metres composed already, which latter is called education, then the difficulty begins, and the good artist is needed. Then the old tale has to be repeated of fair and heavenly love—the love of Urania the fair and heavenly muse, and of the duty of accepting the temperate, and those who are as yet intemperate only that they may become temperate, and of preserving their love; and again, of the vulgar Polyhymnia, who must be used with circumspection that the pleasure be enjoyed, but may not generate licentiousness; just as in my own art it is a great matter so to regulate the desires of the epicure that he may gratify his tastes without the attendant evil of disease. Whence I infer that in music, in medicine, in all other things human as well as divine, both loves ought to be noted as far as may be, for they are both present.

The course of the seasons is also full of both these principles; and when, as I was saying, the elements of hot and cold, moist and dry, attain the harmonious love of one another and blend in temperance and harmony, they bring to men, animals, and plants health and plenty, and do them no harm; whereas the wanton love, getting the upper hand and affecting the seasons of the year, is very destructive and injurious, being the source of pestilence, and bringing many other kinds of diseases on animals and plants; for hoar-frost and hail and blight spring from the excesses and disorders of these elements of love, which to know in relation to the revolutions of the heavenly bodies and the seasons of the year is termed astronomy. Furthermore all sacrifices and the whole province of divination, which is the art of communion between gods and men—these, I say, are concerned only with the preservation of the good and the cure of the evil love. For all manner of impiety is likely to ensue if, instead of accepting and honouring and reverencing the harmonious love in all his actions, a man honours the other love, whether in his feelings towards gods or parents, towards the living or the dead. Wherefore the business of divination is to see to these loves and to heal them, and divination is the peacemaker of gods and men, working by a knowledge of the religious or irreligious tendencies which exist in human loves. Such is the great and mighty, or rather omnipotent force of love in general. And the love, more especially, which is concerned with the good, and which is perfected in company with temperance and justice, whether among gods or men, has the greatest power, and is the source of all our happiness and harmony, and makes us friends with the gods who are above us, and with one another. I dare say that I too have omitted several things which might be said in praise of Love, but this was not intentional, and you, Aristophanes, may now supply the omission or take some other line of commendation; for I perceive that you are rid of the hiccough.

Yes, said Aristophanes, who followed, the hiccough is gone; not, however, until I applied the sneezing; and I wonder whether the harmony of the body has a love of such noises and ticklings, for I no sooner applied the sneezing than I was cured.

Eryximachus said: Beware, friend Aristophanes, although you are going to speak, you are making fun of me;

and I shall have to watch and see whether I cannot have a laugh at your expense, when you might speak in peace.

You are right, said Aristophanes, laughing. I will unsay my words; but do you please not to watch me, as I fear that in the speech which I am about to make, instead of others laughing with me, which is to the manner born of our muse and would be all the better, I shall only be laughed at by them.

Do you expect to shoot your bolt and escape, Aristophanes? Well, perhaps if you are very careful and bear in mind that you will be called to account, I may be induced to let you off.

Aristophanes professed to open another vein of discourse; he had a mind to praise Love in another way, unlike that either of Pausanias or Eryximachus. Mankind, he said, judging by their neglect of him, have never, as I think, at all understood the power of Love. For if they had understood him they would surely have built noble temples and altars, and offered solemn sacrifices in his honour; but this is not done, and most certainly ought to be done: since of all the gods he is the best friend of men, the helper and the healer of the ills which are the great impediment to the happiness of the race. I will try to describe his power to you, and you shall teach the rest of the world what I am teaching you. In the first place, let me treat of the nature of man and what has happened to it; for the original human nature was not like the present, but different. The sexes were not two as they are now, but originally three in number; there was man, woman, and the union of the two, having a name corresponding to this double nature, which had once a real existence, but is now lost, and the word 'Androgynous' is only preserved as a term of reproach. In the second place, the primeval man was round, his back and sides forming a circle; and he had four hands and four feet, one head with two faces, looking opposite ways, set on a round neck and precisely alike; also four ears, two privy members, and the remainder to correspond. He could walk upright as men now do, backwards or forwards as he pleased, and he could also roll over and over at a great pace, turning on his four hands and four feet, eight in all, like tumblers going over and over with their legs in the air; this was when he wanted to run fast. Now the sexes were three, and such as I have described them; because the sun, moon, and earth are three; and the man was originally the child of the sun, the woman of the earth, and the man-woman of the moon, which is made up of sun and earth, and they were all round and moved round and round like their parents. Terrible was their might and strength, and the thoughts of their hearts were great, and they made an attack upon the gods; of them is told the tale of Otys and Ephialtes who, as Homer says, dared to scale heaven, and would have laid hands upon the gods. Doubt reigned in the celestial councils. Should they kill them and annihilate the race with thunderbolts, as they had done the giants, then there would be an end of the sacrifices and worship which men offered to them; but, on the other hand, the gods could not suffer their insolence to be unrestrained. At last, after a good deal of reflection, Zeus discovered a way. He said: 'Methinks I have a plan which will humble their pride and improve their manners; men shall continue to exist, but I will cut them in two and then they will be diminished in strength and increased in numbers; this will have the advantage of making them more profitable to us. They shall walk upright on two legs, and if they continue insolent and will not be quiet, I will split them again and they shall hop about on a single leg.' He spoke and cut men in two, like a sorb-apple which is halved for pickling, or as you might divide an egg with a hair; and as he cut them one after another, he bade Apollo give the face and the half of the neck a turn in order that the man might contemplate the section of himself: he would thus learn a lesson of humility. Apollo was also bidden to heal their wounds and compose their forms. So he gave a turn to the face and pulled the skin from the sides all over that which in our language is called the belly, like the purses which draw in, and he made one mouth at the centre, which he fastened in a knot (the same which is called the navel); he also moulded the breast and took out most of the wrinkles, much as a shoemaker might smooth leather upon a last; he left a few, however, in the region of the belly and navel, as a memorial of the primeval state. After the division the two parts of man, each desiring his other half, came together, and throwing their arms about one another, entwined in mutual embraces, longing to grow into one, they were on the point of dying from hunger and self-neglect, because they did not like to do anything apart; and when one of the halves died and the other survived, the survivor sought another mate, man or woman as we call them,—being the sections of entire men or women,—and clung to that. They were being destroyed, when Zeus in pity of them invented a new plan: he turned the parts of generation round to the front, for this had not been always their position, and they sowed the seed no longer as hitherto like grasshoppers in the ground, but in one another; and after the transposition the male generated in the female in order that by the mutual embraces of man and woman they might breed, and the race might continue; or if man came to man they might be satisfied, and rest, and go their ways to the business of life: so ancient is the desire of one another which is implanted in us, reuniting our original nature, making one of two, and healing the state of man. Each of us when separated, having one side only, like a flat fish, is but the indenture of a man, and he is always looking for his other half. Men who are a section of that double nature which was once called Androgynous are lovers of women; adulterers are generally of this breed, and also adulterous women who lust after men: the women who are a section of the woman do not care for men, but have female attachments; the female companions are of this sort. But they who are a section of the male follow the male, and while they are young, being slices of the original man, they hang about men and embrace them, and they are themselves the best of boys and youths, because they have the most manly nature. Some indeed assert that they are shameless, but this is not true; for they do not act thus from any want of shame, but because they are valiant and manly, and have a manly countenance, and they embrace that which is like them. And these when they grow up become our statesmen, and these only, which is a great proof of the truth of what I am saying. When they reach manhood they are lovers of youth, and are not naturally inclined to marry or beget children,—if at all, they do so only in obedience to the law; but they are satisfied if they may be allowed to live with one another unwedded; and such a nature is prone to love and ready to return love, always embracing that which is akin to him. And when one of them meets with his other half, the actual half of himself, whether he be a lover of youth or a lover of another sort, the pair are lost in an amazement of love and friendship and intimacy, and one will not be out of the other's sight, as I may say, even for a moment: these are the people who pass their whole lives together; yet they could not explain what they desire of one another. For the intense yearning which each of them has towards the other does not appear to be the desire of lover's intercourse, but of something else which the soul of either evidently desires and cannot tell, and of which she has only a dark and doubtful presentiment. Suppose Hephaestus, with his instruments, to come to the pair who are lying side by side and to say to them, 'What do you people want of one another?' they would be unable to explain. And suppose further, that when he saw their perplexity he said: 'Do you desire to be wholly one; always day and night to be in one another's company? for if this is what you desire, I am ready to melt you into one and let you grow together, so that being two you shall become one, and while you live live a common life as if you were a single man, and after your death in the world below still be one departed soul instead of two—I ask whether this is what you lovingly desire, and whether you are satisfied to attain this?'—there is not a man of them who when he heard the proposal would deny or would not acknowledge that this meeting and melting into one another, this becoming one instead of two, was the very expression of his ancient need (compare Arist. Pol.). And the reason is that human nature was originally one and we were a whole, and the desire and pursuit of the whole is called love. There was a time, I say, when we were one, but now because of the wickedness of mankind God has dispersed us, as the Arcadians were dispersed into villages by the Lacedaemonians (compare Arist. Pol.). And if we are not obedient to the gods, there is a danger that we shall be split up again and go about in basso-relievo, like the profile figures having only half a nose which are sculptured on monuments, and that we shall be like tallies. Wherefore let us exhort all men to piety, that we may avoid evil, and obtain the good, of which Love is to us the lord and minister; and let no one oppose him—he is the enemy of the gods who opposes him. For if we are friends of the God and at peace with him we shall find our own true loves, which rarely happens in this world at present. I am serious, and therefore I must beg Eryximachus not to make fun or to find any allusion in what I am saying to Pausanias and Agathon, who, as I suspect, are both of the manly nature, and belong to the class which I have been describing. But my words have a wider application—they include men and women everywhere; and I believe that if our loves were perfectly accomplished, and each one returning to his primeval nature had his original true love, then our race would be happy. And if this would be best of all, the best in the next degree and under present circumstances must be the nearest approach to such an union; and that will be the attainment of a congenial love. Wherefore, if we would praise him who has given to us the benefit, we must praise the god Love, who is our greatest benefactor, both leading us in this life back to our own nature, and giving us high hopes for the future, for he promises that if we are pious, he will restore us to our original state, and heal us and make us happy and blessed. This, Eryximachus, is my discourse of love, which, although different to yours, I must beg you to leave unassailed by the shafts of your ridicule, in order that each may have his turn; each, or rather either, for Agathon and Socrates are the only ones left.

Indeed, I am not going to attack you, said Eryximachus, for I thought your speech charming, and did I not know that Agathon and Socrates are masters in the art of love, I should be really afraid that they would have nothing to say, after the world of things which have been said already. But, for all that, I am not without hopes.

Socrates said: You played your part well, Eryximachus; but if you were as I am now, or rather as I shall be when Agathon has spoken, you would, indeed, be in a great strait.

You want to cast a spell over me, Socrates, said Agathon, in the hope that I may be disconcerted at the expectation raised among the audience that I shall speak well.

I should be strangely forgetful, Agathon replied Socrates, of the courage and magnanimity which you showed when your own compositions were about to be exhibited, and you came upon the stage with the actors and faced the vast theatre altogether undismayed, if I thought that your nerves could be fluttered at a small party of friends.

Do you think, Socrates, said Agathon, that my head is so full of the theatre as not to know how much more formidable to a man of sense a few good judges are than many fools?

Nay, replied Socrates, I should be very wrong in attributing to you, Agathon, that or any other want of refinement. And I am quite aware that if you happened to meet with any whom you thought wise, you would care for their opinion much more than for that of the many. But then we, having been a part of the foolish many in the theatre, cannot be regarded as the select wise; though I know that if you chanced to be in the presence, not of one of ourselves, but of some really wise man, you would be ashamed of disgracing yourself before him—would you not?

Yes, said Agathon.

But before the many you would not be ashamed, if you thought that you were doing something disgraceful in their presence?

Here Phaedrus interrupted them, saying: not answer him, my dear Agathon; for if he can only get a partner with whom he can talk, especially a good-looking one, he will no longer care about the completion of our plan. Now I love to hear him talk; but just at present I must not forget the encomium on Love which I ought to receive from him and from every one. When you and he have paid your tribute to the god, then you may talk.

Very good, Phaedrus, said Agathon; I see no reason why I should not proceed with my speech, as I shall have many other opportunities of conversing with Socrates. Let me say first how I ought to speak, and then speak:—

The previous speakers, instead of praising the god Love, or unfolding his nature, appear to have congratulated mankind on the benefits which he confers upon them. But I would rather praise the god first, and then speak of his gifts; this is always the right way of praising everything. May I say without impiety or offence, that of all the blessed gods he is the most blessed because he is the fairest and best? And he is the fairest: for, in the first place, he is the youngest, and of his youth he is himself the witness, fleeing out of the way of

age, who is swift enough, swifter truly than most of us like:
—Love hates him and will not come near him; but youth
and love live and move together—like to like, as the proverb
says. Many things were said by Phaedrus about Love in
which I agree with him; but I cannot agree that he is older
than Iapetus and Kronos:—not so; I maintain him to be the
youngest of the gods, and youthful ever. The ancient doings
among the gods of which Hesiod and Parmenides spoke, if
the tradition of them be true, were done of Necessity and
not of Love; had Love been in those days, there would have
been no chaining or mutilation of the gods, or other
violence, but peace and sweetness, as there is now in heaven,
since the rule of Love began. Love is young and also tender;
he ought to have a poet like Homer to describe his
tenderness, as Homer says of Ate, that she is a goddess and
tender:—

'Her feet are tender, for she sets her steps, Not on the
ground but on the heads of men:'

herein is an excellent proof of her tenderness,—that she
walks not upon the hard but upon the soft. Let us adduce a
similar proof of the tenderness of Love; for he walks not
upon the earth, nor yet upon the skulls of men, which are
not so very soft, but in the hearts and souls of both gods and
men, which are of all things the softest: in them he walks
and dwells and makes his home. Not in every soul without
exception, for where there is hardness he departs, where
there is softness there he dwells; and nestling always with his
feet and in all manner of ways in the softest of soft places,
how can he be other than the softest of all things? Of a
truth he is the tenderest as well as the youngest, and also he
is of flexile form; for if he were hard and without flexure he

could not enfold all things, or wind his way into and out of every soul of man undiscovered. And a proof of his flexibility and symmetry of form is his grace, which is universally admitted to be in an especial manner the attribute of Love; ungrace and love are always at war with one another. The fairness of his complexion is revealed by his habitation among the flowers; for he dwells not amid bloomless or fading beauties, whether of body or soul or aught else, but in the place of flowers and scents, there he sits and abides. Concerning the beauty of the god I have said enough; and yet there remains much more which I might say. Of his virtue I have now to speak: his greatest glory is that he can neither do nor suffer wrong to or from any god or any man; for he suffers not by force if he suffers; force comes not near him, neither when he acts does he act by force. For all men in all things serve him of their own free will, and where there is voluntary agreement, there, as the laws which are the lords of the city say, is justice. And not only is he just but exceedingly temperate, for Temperance is the acknowledged ruler of the pleasures and desires, and no pleasure ever masters Love; he is their master and they are his servants; and if he conquers them he must be temperate indeed. As to courage, even the God of War is no match for him; he is the captive and Love is the lord, for love, the love of Aphrodite, masters him, as the tale runs; and the master is stronger than the servant. And if he conquers the bravest of all others, he must be himself the bravest. Of his courage and justice and temperance I have spoken, but I have yet to speak of his wisdom; and according to the measure of my ability I must try to do my best. In the first place he is a poet (and here, like Eryximachus, I magnify my art), and he is also the source of poesy in others, which he could not be if he were not himself a poet. And at the touch of him every one becomes a poet, even though he had no music in him before (A fragment of the Sthenoaoea of Euripides.); this also is a proof that Love is a good poet and accomplished in all the fine arts; for no one can give to another that which he has not himself, or teach that of which he has no knowledge. Who will deny that the creation of the animals is his doing? Are they not all the works of his wisdom, born and begotten of him? And as to the artists, do we not know that he only of them whom love inspires has the light of fame?—he whom Love touches not walks in darkness. The arts of medicine and archery and divination were discovered by Apollo, under the guidance of love and desire; so that he too is a disciple of Love. Also the melody of the Muses, the metallurgy of Hephaestus, the weaving of Athene, the empire of Zeus over gods and men, are all due to Love, who was the inventor of them. And so Love set in order the empire of the gods—the love of beauty, as is evident, for with deformity Love has no concern. In the days of old, as I began by saying, dreadful deeds were done among the gods, for they were ruled by Necessity; but now since the birth of Love, and from the Love of the beautiful, has sprung every good in heaven and earth. Therefore, Phaedrus, I say of Love that he is the fairest and best in himself, and the cause of what is fairest and best in all other things. And there comes into my mind a line of poetry in which he is said to be the god who

'Gives peace on earth and calms the stormy deep, Who stills the winds and bids the sufferer sleep.'

This is he who empties men of disaffection and fills

them with affection, who makes them to meet together at banquets such as these: in sacrifices, feasts, dances, he is our lord—who sends courtesy and sends away discourtesy, who gives kindness ever and never gives unkindness; the friend of the good, the wonder of the wise, the amazement of the gods; desired by those who have no part in him, and precious to those who have the better part in him; parent of delicacy, luxury, desire, fondness, softness, grace; regardful of the good, regardless of the evil: in every word, work, wish, fear—saviour, pilot, comrade, helper; glory of gods and men, leader best and brightest: in whose footsteps let every man follow, sweetly singing in his honour and joining in that sweet strain with which love charms the souls of gods and men. Such is the speech, Phaedrus, half-playful, yet having a certain measure of seriousness, which, according to my ability, I dedicate to the god.

When Agathon had done speaking, Aristodemus said that there was a general cheer; the young man was thought to have spoken in a manner worthy of himself, and of the god. And Socrates, looking at Eryximachus, said: Tell me, son of Acumenus, was there not reason in my fears? and was I not a true prophet when I said that Agathon would make a wonderful oration, and that I should be in a strait?

The part of the prophecy which concerns Agathon, replied Eryximachus, appears to me to be true; but not the other part—that you will be in a strait.

Why, my dear friend, said Socrates, must not I or any one be in a strait who has to speak after he has heard such a rich and varied discourse? I am especially struck with the beauty of the concluding words—who could listen to them without amazement? When I reflected on the immeasurable inferiority of my own powers, I was ready to run away for shame, if there had been a possibility of escape. For I was reminded of Gorgias, and at the end of his speech I fancied that Agathon was shaking at me the Gorginian or Gorgonian head of the great master of rhetoric, which was simply to turn me and my speech into stone, as Homer says (Odyssey), and strike me dumb. And then I perceived how foolish I had been in consenting to take my turn with you in praising love, and saying that I too was a master of the art, when I really had no conception how anything ought to be praised. For in my simplicity I imagined that the topics of praise should be true, and that this being presupposed, out of the true the speaker was to choose the best and set them forth in the best manner. And I felt quite proud, thinking that I knew the nature of true praise, and should speak well. Whereas I now see that the intention was to attribute to Love every species of greatness and glory, whether really belonging to him or not, without regard to truth or falsehood—that was no matter; for the original proposal seems to have been not that each of you should really praise Love, but only that you should appear to praise him. And so you attribute to Love every imaginable form of praise which can be gathered anywhere; and you say that 'he is all this,' and 'the cause of all that,' making him appear the fairest and best of all to those who know him not, for you cannot impose upon those who know him. And a noble and solemn hymn of praise have you rehearsed. But as I misunderstood the nature of the praise when I said that I would take my turn, I must beg to be absolved from the promise which I made in ignorance, and which (as Euripides would say (Eurip. Hyppolytus)) was a promise of the lips and not of the mind. Farewell then to such a strain: for I do not praise in that way; no, indeed, I cannot. But if you like to hear the truth about love, I am ready to speak in my own manner, though I will not make myself ridiculous by entering into any rivalry with you. Say then, Phaedrus, whether you would like to have the truth about love, spoken in any words and in any order which may happen to come into my mind at the time. Will that be agreeable to you?

Aristodemus said that Phaedrus and the company bid him speak in any manner which he thought best. Then, he added, let me have your permission first to ask Agathon a few more questions, in order that I may take his admissions as the premises of my discourse.

I grant the permission, said Phaedrus: put your questions. Socrates then proceeded as follows:—

In the magnificent oration which you have just uttered, I think that you were right, my dear Agathon, in proposing to speak of the nature of Love first and afterwards of his works —that is a way of beginning which I very much approve. And as you have spoken so eloquently of his nature, may I ask you further, Whether love is the love of something or of nothing? And here I must explain myself: I do not want you to say that love is the love of a father or the love of a mother —that would be ridiculous; but to answer as you would, if I asked is a father a father of something? to which you would find no difficulty in replying, of a son or daughter: and the answer would be right.

Very true, said Agathon.

And you would say the same of a mother?

He assented.

Yet let me ask you one more question in order to

illustrate my meaning: Is not a brother to be regarded essentially as a brother of something?

Certainly, he replied.

That is, of a brother or sister?

Yes, he said.

And now, said Socrates, I will ask about Love:—Is Love of something or of nothing?

Of something, surely, he replied.

Keep in mind what this is, and tell me what I want to know—whether Love desires that of which love is.

Yes, surely.

And does he possess, or does he not possess, that which he loves and desires?

Probably not, I should say.

Nay, replied Socrates, I would have you consider whether 'necessarily' is not rather the word. The inference that he who desires something is in want of something, and that he who desires nothing is in want of nothing, is in my judgment, Agathon, absolutely and necessarily true. What do you think?

I agree with you, said Agathon.

Very good. Would he who is great, desire to be great, or he who is strong, desire to be strong?

That would be inconsistent with our previous admissions.

True. For he who is anything cannot want to be that which he is?

Very true.

And yet, added Socrates, if a man being strong desired to be strong, or being swift desired to be swift, or being healthy desired to be healthy, in that case he might be thought to desire something which he already has or is. I give the example in order that we may avoid misconception. For the possessors of these qualities, Agathon, must be supposed to have their respective advantages at the time, whether they choose or not; and who can desire that which he has? Therefore, when a person says, I am well and wish to be well, or I am rich and wish to be rich, and I desire simply to have what I have—to him we shall reply: 'You, my friend, having wealth and health and strength, want to have the continuance of them; for at this moment, whether you choose or no, you have them. And when you say, I desire that which I have and nothing else, is not your meaning that you want to have what you now have in the future?' He must agree with us—must he not?

He must, replied Agathon.

Then, said Socrates, he desires that what he has at present may be preserved to him in the future, which is equivalent to saying that he desires something which is non-existent to him, and which as yet he has not got:

Very true, he said.

Then he and every one who desires, desires that which he has not already, and which is future and not present, and which he has not, and is not, and of which he is in want;— these are the sort of things which love and desire seek?

Very true, he said.

Then now, said Socrates, let us recapitulate the argument. First, is not love of something, and of something too which is wanting to a man?

Yes, he replied.

Remember further what you said in your speech, or if you do not remember I will remind you: you said that the love of the beautiful set in order the empire of the gods, for that of deformed things there is no love—did you not say something of that kind?

Yes, said Agathon.

Yes, my friend, and the remark was a just one. And if this is true, Love is the love of beauty and not of deformity?

He assented.

And the admission has been already made that Love is of something which a man wants and has not?

True, he said.

Then Love wants and has not beauty?

Certainly, he replied.

And would you call that beautiful which wants and does not possess beauty?

Certainly not.

Then would you still say that love is beautiful?

Agathon replied: I fear that I did not understand what I was saying.

You made a very good speech, Agathon, replied Socrates; but there is yet one small question which I would fain ask:—Is not the good also the beautiful?

Yes.

Then in wanting the beautiful, love wants also the good?

I cannot refute you, Socrates, said Agathon:—Let us assume that what you say is true.

Say rather, beloved Agathon, that you cannot refute the truth; for Socrates is easily refuted.

And now, taking my leave of you, I would rehearse a tale of love which I heard from Diotima of Mantineia (compare 1 Alcibiades), a woman wise in this and in many other kinds of knowledge, who in the days of old, when the Athenians offered sacrifice before the coming of the plague, delayed the disease ten years. She was my instructress in the art of love, and I shall repeat to you what she said to me, beginning with the admissions made by Agathon, which are nearly if not quite the same which I made to the wise woman when she questioned me: I think that this will be the easiest way, and I shall take both parts myself as well as I can (compare Gorgias). As you, Agathon, suggested (supra), I must speak first of the being and nature of Love, and then of his works. First I said to her in nearly the same words which he used to me, that Love was a mighty god, and likewise fair; and she proved to me as I proved to him that, by my own showing, Love was neither fair nor good. 'What do you mean, Diotima,' I said, 'is love then evil and foul?' 'Hush,' she cried; 'must that be foul which is not fair?' 'Certainly,' I said. 'And is that which is not wise, ignorant? do you not see that there is a mean between wisdom and ignorance?' 'And what may that be?' I said. 'Right opinion,' she replied; 'which, as you know, being incapable of giving a reason, is not knowledge (for how can knowledge be devoid of reason? nor again, ignorance, for neither can ignorance attain the truth), but is clearly something which is a mean between ignorance and wisdom.' 'Quite true,' I replied. 'Do not then insist,' she said, 'that what is not fair is of necessity foul, or what is not good evil; or infer that because love is not fair and good he is therefore foul and evil; for he is in a mean between them.' 'Well,' I said, 'Love is surely admitted by all to be a great god.' 'By those who know or by those who do not know?' 'By all.' 'And how, Socrates,' she said with a smile, 'can Love be acknowledged to be a great god by those who say that he is not a god at all?' 'And who are they?' I said. 'You and I are two of them,' she replied. 'How can that be?' I said. 'It is quite intelligible,' she replied; 'for you yourself would acknowledge that the gods are happy and fair—of course you would—would you dare to say that any god was not?' 'Certainly not,' I replied. 'And you mean by the happy, those who are the possessors of things good or fair?' 'Yes.' 'And you admitted that Love, because he was in want, desires those good and fair things of which he is in want?' 'Yes, I did.' 'But how can he be a god who has no portion in what is either good or fair?' 'Impossible.' 'Then you see that you also deny the divinity of Love.'

'What then is Love?' I asked; 'Is he mortal?' 'No.' 'What then?' 'As in the former instance, he is neither mortal nor immortal, but in a mean between the two.' 'What is he, Diotima?' 'He is a great spirit (daimon), and like all spirits he is intermediate between the divine and the mortal.' 'And what,' I said, 'is his power?' 'He interprets,' she replied, 'between gods and men, conveying and taking across to the gods the prayers and sacrifices of men, and to men the commands and replies of the gods; he is the mediator who spans the chasm which divides them, and therefore in him all is bound together, and through him the arts of the prophet and the priest, their sacrifices and mysteries and charms, and all prophecy and incantation, find their way. For God mingles not with man; but through Love all the intercourse and converse of God with man, whether awake or asleep, is carried on. The wisdom which understands this is spiritual; all other wisdom, such as that of arts and handicrafts, is mean and vulgar. Now these spirits or intermediate powers are many and diverse, and one of them is Love.' 'And who,' I said, 'was his father, and who his mother?' 'The tale,' she said, 'will take time; nevertheless I will tell you. On the birthday of Aphrodite there was a feast of the gods, at which the god Poros or Plenty, who is the son of Metis or Discretion, was one of the guests. When the feast was over, Penia or Poverty, as the manner is on such occasions, came about the doors to beg. Now Plenty who was the worse for nectar (there was no wine in those days), went into the garden of Zeus and fell into a heavy sleep, and Poverty considering her own straitened circumstances, plotted to have a child by him, and accordingly she lay down at his side and conceived Love, who partly because he is naturally a lover of the beautiful, and because Aphrodite is herself beautiful, and also because he was born on her birthday, is her follower and attendant. And as his parentage is, so also are his fortunes. In the first place he is always poor, and anything but tender and fair, as the many imagine him; and he is rough and squalid, and has no shoes, nor a house to dwell in; on the bare earth exposed he lies under the open heaven, in the streets, or at the doors of houses, taking his rest; and like his mother he is always in distress. Like his father too, whom he also partly resembles, he is always plotting against the fair and good; he is bold, enterprising, strong, a mighty hunter, always weaving some intrigue or other, keen in the pursuit of wisdom, fertile in resources; a philosopher at all times, terrible as an enchanter, sorcerer, sophist. He is by nature neither mortal nor immortal, but alive and flourishing at one moment when he is in plenty, and dead at another moment, and again alive by reason of his father's nature. But that which is always flowing in is always flowing out, and so he is never in want and never in wealth; and, further, he is in a mean between ignorance and knowledge. The truth of the matter is this: No god is a philosopher or seeker after wisdom, for he is wise already; nor does any man who is wise seek after wisdom. Neither do the ignorant seek after wisdom. For herein is the evil of ignorance, that he who is neither good nor wise is nevertheless satisfied with himself: he has no desire for that of which he feels no want.' 'But who then, Diotima,' I said, 'are the lovers of wisdom, if they are neither the wise nor the foolish?' 'A child may answer that question,' she replied; 'they are those who are in a mean between the two; Love is one of them. For wisdom is a most beautiful thing, and Love is of the beautiful; and therefore Love is also a philosopher or lover of wisdom, and being a lover of wisdom is in a mean between the wise and the ignorant. And of this too his birth is the cause; for his father is wealthy and wise, and his mother poor and foolish. Such, my dear Socrates, is the nature of the spirit Love. The error in your conception of him was very natural, and as I imagine from what you say, has arisen out of a confusion of love and the beloved, which made you think that love was all beautiful. For the beloved is the truly beautiful, and delicate, and perfect, and blessed; but the principle of love is of another nature, and is such as I have described.'

I said, 'O thou stranger woman, thou sayest well; but, assuming Love to be such as you say, what is the use of him to men?' 'That, Socrates,' she replied, 'I will attempt to unfold: of his nature and birth I have already spoken; and you acknowledge that love is of the beautiful. But some one will say: Of the beautiful in what, Socrates and Diotima?— or rather let me put the question more clearly, and ask: When a man loves the beautiful, what does he desire?' I answered her 'That the beautiful may be his.' 'Still,' she said, 'the answer suggests a further question: What is given by the possession of beauty?' 'To what you have asked,' I replied, 'I have no answer ready.' 'Then,' she said, 'let me put the word "good" in the place of the beautiful, and repeat the question once more: If he who loves loves the good, what is it then that he loves?' 'The possession of the good,' I said. 'And what does he gain who possesses the good?' 'Happiness,' I replied; 'there is less difficulty in answering that question.' 'Yes,' she said, 'the happy are made happy by the acquisition of good things. Nor is there any need to ask why a man desires happiness; the answer is already final.' 'You are right.' I said. 'And is this wish and this desire common to all? and do all men always desire their own good, or only some men?—what say you?' 'All men,' I replied; 'the desire is common to all.' 'Why, then,' she rejoined, 'are not all men, Socrates, said to love, but only some of them? whereas you say that all men are always loving the same things.' 'I myself wonder,' I said, 'why this is.' 'There is nothing to wonder at,' she replied; 'the reason is that one part of love is separated off and receives the name of the whole, but the other parts have other names.' 'Give an illustration,' I said. She answered me as follows: 'There is poetry, which, as you know, is complex and manifold. All creation or passage of non-being into being is poetry or making, and the processes of all art are creative; and the masters of arts are all poets or makers.' 'Very true.' 'Still,' she said, 'you know that they are not called poets, but have other names; only that portion of the art which is separated off from the rest, and is concerned with music and metre, is termed poetry, and they who possess poetry in this sense of the word are called poets.' 'Very true,' I said. 'And the same holds of love. For you may say generally that all desire of good and happiness is only the great and subtle power of love; but they who are drawn towards him by any other path, whether the path of money-making or gymnastics or philosophy, are not called lovers—the name of the whole is appropriated to those whose affection takes one form only—they alone are said to love, or to be lovers.' 'I dare say,' I replied, 'that you are right.' 'Yes,' she added, 'and you hear people say that lovers are seeking for their other half; but I say that they are seeking neither for the half of themselves, nor for the whole, unless the half or the whole be also a good. And they will cut off their own hands and feet and cast them away, if they are evil; for they love not what is their own, unless perchance there be some one who calls what belongs to him the good, and what belongs to another the evil. For there is nothing which men love but the good. Is there anything?' 'Certainly, I should say, that there is nothing.' 'Then,' she said, 'the simple truth is, that men love the good.' 'Yes,' I said. 'To which must be added that they love the possession of the good?' 'Yes, that must be added.' 'And not only the possession, but the everlasting possession of the good?' 'That must be added too.' 'Then love,' she said, 'may be described generally as the love of the everlasting possession of the good?' 'That is most true.'

'Then if this be the nature of love, can you tell me further,' she said, 'what is the manner of the pursuit? what are they doing who show all this eagerness and heat which is called love? and what is the object which they have in view? Answer me.' 'Nay, Diotima,' I replied, 'if I had known, I should not have wondered at your wisdom, neither should I have come to learn from you about this very matter.' 'Well,' she said, 'I will teach you:—The object which they have in view is birth in beauty, whether of body or soul.' 'I do not understand you,' I said; 'the oracle requires an explanation.' 'I will make my meaning clearer,' she replied. 'I mean to say, that all men are bringing to the birth in their bodies and in their souls. There is a certain age at which human nature is desirous of procreation—procreation which must be in beauty and not in deformity; and this procreation is the union of man and woman, and is a divine thing; for conception and generation are an immortal principle in the mortal creature, and in the inharmonious they can never be. But the deformed is always inharmonious with the divine, and the beautiful harmonious. Beauty, then, is the destiny or goddess of parturition who presides at birth, and therefore, when approaching beauty, the conceiving power is propitious, and diffusive, and benign, and begets and bears fruit: at the sight of ugliness she frowns and contracts and has a sense of pain, and turns away, and shrivels up, and not without a pang refrains from conception. And this is the reason why, when the hour of conception arrives, and the teeming nature is full, there is such a flutter and ecstasy about beauty whose approach is the alleviation of the pain of travail. For love, Socrates, is not, as you imagine, the love of the beautiful only.' 'What then?' 'The love of generation and of birth in beauty.' 'Yes,' I said. 'Yes, indeed,' she replied. 'But why of generation?' 'Because to the mortal creature, generation is a sort of eternity and immortality,' she replied; 'and if, as has been already admitted, love is of the everlasting possession of the good, all men will necessarily desire immortality together with good: Wherefore love is of immortality.'

All this she taught me at various times when she spoke of love. And I remember her once saying to me, 'What is the cause, Socrates, of love, and the attendant desire? See you not how all animals, birds, as well as beasts, in their desire of procreation, are in agony when they take the infection of love, which begins with the desire of union; whereto is added the care of offspring, on whose behalf the weakest are ready to battle against the strongest even to the uttermost, and to die for them, and will let themselves be tormented with hunger or suffer anything in order to maintain their young. Man may be supposed to act thus from reason; but why should animals have these passionate feelings? Can you tell me why?' Again I replied that I did not know. She said to me: 'And do you expect ever to become a master in the art of love, if you do not know this?' 'But I have told you already, Diotima, that my ignorance is the reason why I come to you; for I am conscious that I want a teacher; tell me then the cause of this and of the other mysteries of love.' 'Marvel not,' she said, 'if you believe that love is of the immortal, as we have several times acknowledged; for here again, and on the same principle too, the mortal nature is seeking as far as is possible to be everlasting and immortal: and this is only to be attained by generation, because generation always leaves behind a new existence in the place of the old. Nay even in the life of the same individual there is succession and not absolute unity: a man is called the same, and yet in the short interval which elapses between youth and age, and in which every animal is said to have life and identity, he is undergoing a perpetual process of loss and reparation—hair, flesh, bones, blood, and the whole body are always changing. Which is true not only of the body, but also of the soul, whose habits, tempers, opinions, desires, pleasures, pains, fears, never remain the same in any one of us, but are always coming and going; and equally true of knowledge, and what is still more surprising to us mortals, not only do the sciences in general spring up and decay, so that in respect of them we are never the same; but each of them individually experiences a like change. For what is implied in the word "recollection," but the departure of knowledge, which is ever being forgotten, and is renewed and preserved by recollection, and appears to be the same although in reality new, according to that law of succession by which all mortal things are preserved, not absolutely the same, but by substitution, the old worn-out mortality leaving another new and similar existence behind —unlike the divine, which is always the same and not another? And in this way, Socrates, the mortal body, or mortal anything, partakes of immortality; but the immortal in another way. Marvel not then at the love which all men have of their offspring; for that universal love and interest is for the sake of immortality.'

I was astonished at her words, and said: 'Is this really true, O thou wise Diotima?' And she answered with all the authority of an accomplished sophist: 'Of that, Socrates, you may be assured;—think only of the ambition of men, and you will wonder at the senselessness of their ways, unless you consider how they are stirred by the love of an immortality of fame. They are ready to run all risks greater far than they would have run for their children, and to spend money and undergo any sort of toil, and even to die, for the sake of leaving behind them a name which shall be eternal. Do you imagine that Alcestis would have died to save Admetus, or Achilles to avenge Patroclus, or your own Codrus in order to preserve the kingdom for his sons, if they had not imagined that the memory of their virtues, which still survives among us, would be immortal? Nay,' she said, 'I am persuaded that all men do all things, and the better they are the more they do them, in hope of the glorious fame of immortal virtue; for they desire the immortal.

'Those who are pregnant in the body only, betake themselves to women and beget children—this is the character of their love; their offspring, as they hope, will preserve their memory and giving them the blessedness and immortality which they desire in the future. But souls which are pregnant—for there certainly are men who are more creative in their souls than in their bodies—conceive that which is proper for the soul to conceive or contain. And what are these conceptions?—wisdom and virtue in general. And such creators are poets and all artists who are deserving of the name inventor. But the greatest and fairest sort of wisdom by far is that which is concerned with the ordering of states and families, and which is called temperance and justice. And he who in youth has the seed of these implanted in him and is himself inspired, when he comes to maturity desires to beget and generate. He wanders about seeking beauty that he may beget offspring—for in deformity he will beget nothing—and naturally embraces the beautiful rather than the deformed body; above all when he finds a fair and noble and well-nurtured soul, he embraces the two in one person, and to such an one he is full of speech about virtue and the nature and pursuits of a good man; and he tries to educate him; and at the touch of the beautiful which is ever present to his memory, even when absent, he brings forth that which he had conceived long before, and in company with him tends that which he brings forth; and they are married by a far nearer tie and have a closer friendship than those who beget mortal children, for the children who are their common offspring are fairer and more immortal. Who, when he thinks of Homer and Hesiod and other great poets, would not rather have their children than ordinary human ones? Who would not emulate them in the creation of children such as theirs, which have preserved their memory and given them everlasting glory? Or who would not have such children as Lycurgus left behind him to be the saviours, not only of Lacedaemon, but of Hellas, as one may say? There is Solon, too, who is the revered father of Athenian laws; and many others there are in many other places, both among Hellenes and barbarians, who have given to the world many noble works, and have been the parents of virtue of every kind; and many temples have been raised in their honour for the sake of children such as theirs; which were never raised in honour of any one, for the sake of his mortal children.

'These are the lesser mysteries of love, into which even you, Socrates, may enter; to the greater and more hidden ones which are the crown of these, and to which, if you pursue them in a right spirit, they will lead, I know not whether you will be able to attain. But I will do my utmost to inform you, and do you follow if you can. For he who would proceed aright in this matter should begin in youth to visit beautiful forms; and first, if he be guided by his instructor aright, to love one such form only—out of that he should create fair thoughts; and soon he will of himself perceive that the beauty of one form is akin to the beauty of another; and then if beauty of form in general is his pursuit, how foolish would he be not to recognize that the beauty in every form is and the same! And when he perceives this he will abate his violent love of the one, which he will despise and deem a small thing, and will become a lover of all beautiful forms; in the next stage he will consider that the beauty of the mind is more honourable than the beauty of the outward form. So that if a virtuous soul have but a little comeliness, he will be content to love and tend him, and will search out and bring to the birth thoughts which may improve the young, until he is compelled to contemplate and see the beauty of institutions and laws, and to understand that the beauty of them all is of one family, and that personal beauty is a trifle; and after laws and institutions he will go on to the sciences, that he may see their beauty, being not like a servant in love with the beauty of one youth or man or institution, himself a slave mean and narrow-minded, but drawing towards and contemplating the vast sea of beauty, he will create many fair and noble thoughts and notions in boundless love of wisdom; until on that shore he grows and waxes strong, and at last the vision is revealed to him of a single science, which is the science of beauty everywhere. To this I will proceed; please to give me your very best attention:

'He who has been instructed thus far in the things of love, and who has learned to see the beautiful in due order and succession, when he comes toward the end will suddenly perceive a nature of wondrous beauty (and this, Socrates, is the final cause of all our former toils)—a nature which in the first place is everlasting, not growing and decaying, or waxing and waning; secondly, not fair in one point of view and foul in another, or at one time or in one relation or at one place fair, at another time or in another relation or at another place foul, as if fair to some and foul to others, or in the likeness of a face or hands or any other part of the bodily frame, or in any form of speech or knowledge, or existing in any other being, as for example, in an animal, or in heaven, or in earth, or in any other place; but beauty absolute, separate, simple, and everlasting, which without diminution and without increase, or any change, is imparted to the ever-growing and perishing beauties of all other things. He who from these ascending under the influence of true love, begins to perceive that beauty, is not far from the end. And the true order of going, or being led by another, to the things of love, is to begin from the beauties of earth and mount upwards for the sake of that other beauty, using these as steps only, and from one going on to two, and from two to all fair forms, and from fair forms to fair practices, and from fair practices to fair notions, until from fair notions he arrives at the notion of absolute beauty, and at last knows what the essence of beauty is. This, my dear Socrates,' said the stranger of Mantineia, 'is that life above all others which man should live, in the contemplation of beauty absolute; a beauty which if you once beheld, you would see not to be after the measure of gold, and garments, and fair boys and youths, whose presence now entrances you; and you and many a one would be content to live seeing them only and conversing with them without meat or drink, if that were possible—you only want to look at them and to be with them. But what if man had eyes to see the true beauty—the divine beauty, I mean, pure and clear and unalloyed, not clogged with the pollutions of mortality and all the colours and vanities of human life—thither looking, and holding converse with the true beauty simple and divine? Remember how in that communion only, beholding beauty with the eye of the mind, he will be enabled to bring forth, not images of beauty, but realities (for he has hold not of an image but of a reality), and bringing forth and nourishing true virtue to become the friend of God and be immortal, if mortal man may. Would that be an ignoble life?'

Such, Phaedrus—and I speak not only to you, but to all of you—were the words of Diotima; and I am persuaded of their truth. And being persuaded of them, I try to persuade others, that in the attainment of this end human nature will not easily find a helper better than love: And therefore, also, I say that every man ought to honour him as I myself honour him, and walk in his ways, and exhort others to do the same, and praise the power and spirit of love according to the measure of my ability now and ever.

The words which I have spoken, you, Phaedrus, may call an encomium of love, or anything else which you please.

When Socrates had done speaking, the company applauded, and Aristophanes was beginning to say something in answer to the allusion which Socrates had made to his own speech, when suddenly there was a great knocking at the door of the house, as of revellers, and the sound of a flute-girl was heard. Agathon told the attendants to go and see who were the intruders. 'If they are friends of ours,' he said, 'invite them in, but if not, say that the drinking is over.' A little while afterwards they heard the voice of Alcibiades resounding in the court; he was in a great state of intoxication, and kept roaring and shouting 'Where is Agathon? Lead me to Agathon,' and at length, supported by the flute-girl and some of his attendants, he found his way to them. 'Hail, friends,' he said, appearing at the door crowned with a massive garland of ivy and violets, his head flowing with ribands. 'Will you have a very drunken man as a companion of your revels? Or shall I crown Agathon, which was my intention in coming, and go away? For I was unable to come yesterday, and therefore I am here to-day, carrying on my head these ribands, that taking them from my own head, I may crown the head of this fairest and wisest of men, as I may be allowed to call him. Will you laugh at me because I am drunk? Yet I know very well that I am speaking the truth, although you may laugh. But first tell me; if I come in shall we have the understanding of which I spoke (supra Will you have a very drunken man? etc.)? Will you drink with me or not?'

The company were vociferous in begging that he would take his place among them, and Agathon specially invited him. Thereupon he was led in by the people who were with him; and as he was being led, intending to crown Agathon, he took the ribands from his own head and held them in front of his eyes; he was thus prevented from seeing Socrates, who made way for him, and Alcibiades took the vacant place between Agathon and Socrates, and in taking the place he embraced Agathon and crowned him. Take off his sandals, said Agathon, and let him make a third on the same couch.

By all means; but who makes the third partner in our revels? said Alcibiades, turning round and starting up as he caught sight of Socrates. By Heracles, he said, what is this? here is Socrates always lying in wait for me, and always, as his way is, coming out at all sorts of unsuspected places: and now, what have you to say for yourself, and why are you lying here, where I perceive that you have contrived to find a place, not by a joker or lover of jokes, like Aristophanes, but by the fairest of the company?

Socrates turned to Agathon and said: I must ask you to protect me, Agathon; for the passion of this man has grown quite a serious matter to me. Since I became his admirer I have never been allowed to speak to any other fair one, or so much as to look at them. If I do, he goes wild with envy and jealousy, and not only abuses me but can hardly keep his hands off me, and at this moment he may do me some harm. Please to see to this, and either reconcile me to him, or, if he attempts violence, protect me, as I am in bodily fear of his mad and passionate attempts.

There can never be reconciliation between you and me, said Alcibiades; but for the present I will defer your chastisement. And I must beg you, Agathon, to give me back some of the ribands that I may crown the marvellous head of this universal despot—I would not have him complain of me for crowning you, and neglecting him, who in conversation is the conqueror of all mankind; and this not only once, as you were the day before yesterday, but always. Whereupon, taking some of the ribands, he crowned Socrates, and again reclined.

Then he said: You seem, my friends, to be sober, which is a thing not to be endured; you must drink—for that was the agreement under which I was admitted—and I elect myself master of the feast until you are well drunk. Let us have a large goblet, Agathon, or rather, he said, addressing the attendant, bring me that wine-cooler. The wine-cooler which had caught his eye was a vessel holding more than two quarts—this he filled and emptied, and bade the attendant fill it again for Socrates. Observe, my friends, said Alcibiades, that this ingenious trick of mine will have no effect on Socrates, for he can drink any quantity of wine and not be at all nearer being drunk. Socrates drank the cup which the attendant filled for him.

Eryximachus said: What is this, Alcibiades? Are we to have neither conversation nor singing over our cups; but simply to drink as if we were thirsty?

Alcibiades replied: Hail, worthy son of a most wise and worthy sire!

The same to you, said Eryximachus; but what shall we do?

That I leave to you, said Alcibiades.

'The wise physician skilled our wounds to heal (from Pope's Homer, Il.)'

shall prescribe and we will obey. What do you want?

Well, said Eryximachus, before you appeared we had passed a resolution that each one of us in turn should make a speech in praise of love, and as good a one as he could: the turn was passed round from left to right; and as all of us have spoken, and you have not spoken but have well drunken, you ought to speak, and then impose upon Socrates any task which you please, and he on his right hand neighbour, and so on.

That is good, Eryximachus, said Alcibiades; and yet the comparison of a drunken man's speech with those of sober men is hardly fair; and I should like to know, sweet friend, whether you really believe what Socrates was just now saying; for I can assure you that the very reverse is the fact, and that if I praise any one but himself in his presence, whether God or man, he will hardly keep his hands off me.

For shame, said Socrates.

Hold your tongue, said Alcibiades, for by Poseidon, there is no one else whom I will praise when you are of the company.

Well then, said Eryximachus, if you like praise Socrates.

What do you think, Eryximachus? said Alcibiades: shall I attack him and inflict the punishment before you all?

What are you about? said Socrates; are you going to raise a laugh at my expense? Is that the meaning of your praise?

I am going to speak the truth, if you will permit me.

I not only permit, but exhort you to speak the truth.

Then I will begin at once, said Alcibiades, and if I say anything which is not true, you may interrupt me if you will, and say 'that is a lie,' though my intention is to speak the truth. But you must not wonder if I speak any how as things come into my mind; for the fluent and orderly enumeration of all your singularities is not a task which is easy to a man in my condition.

And now, my boys, I shall praise Socrates in a figure which will appear to him to be a caricature, and yet I speak, not to make fun of him, but only for the truth's sake. I say, that he is exactly like the busts of Silenus, which are set up in the statuaries' shops, holding pipes and flutes in their mouths; and they are made to open in the middle, and have images of gods inside them. I say also that he is like Marsyas the satyr. You yourself will not deny, Socrates, that your face

is like that of a satyr. Aye, and there is a resemblance in
other points too. For example, you are a bully, as I can prove
by witnesses, if you will not confess. And are you not a flute-
player? That you are, and a performer far more wonderful
than Marsyas. He indeed with instruments used to charm
the souls of men by the power of his breath, and the players
of his music do so still: for the melodies of Olympus
(compare Arist. Pol.) are derived from Marsyas who taught
them, and these, whether they are played by a great master
or by a miserable flute-girl, have a power which no others
have; they alone possess the soul and reveal the wants of
those who have need of gods and mysteries, because they
are divine. But you produce the same effect with your words
only, and do not require the flute: that is the difference
between you and him. When we hear any other speaker,
even a very good one, he produces absolutely no effect upon
us, or not much, whereas the mere fragments of you and
your words, even at second-hand, and however imperfectly
repeated, amaze and possess the souls of every man,
woman, and child who comes within hearing of them. And
if I were not afraid that you would think me hopelessly
drunk, I would have sworn as well as spoken to the influence
which they have always had and still have over me. For my
heart leaps within me more than that of any Corybantian
reveller, and my eyes rain tears when I hear them. And I
observe that many others are affected in the same manner. I
have heard Pericles and other great orators, and I thought
that they spoke well, but I never had any similar feeling; my
soul was not stirred by them, nor was I angry at the thought
of my own slavish state. But this Marsyas has often brought
me to such a pass, that I have felt as if I could hardly endure

the life which I am leading (this, Socrates, you will admit); and I am conscious that if I did not shut my ears against him, and fly as from the voice of the siren, my fate would be like that of others,—he would transfix me, and I should grow old sitting at his feet. For he makes me confess that I ought not to live as I do, neglecting the wants of my own soul, and busying myself with the concerns of the Athenians; therefore I hold my ears and tear myself away from him. And he is the only person who ever made me ashamed, which you might think not to be in my nature, and there is no one else who does the same. For I know that I cannot answer him or say that I ought not to do as he bids, but when I leave his presence the love of popularity gets the better of me. And therefore I run away and fly from him, and when I see him I am ashamed of what I have confessed to him. Many a time have I wished that he were dead, and yet I know that I should be much more sorry than glad, if he were to die: so that I am at my wit's end.

And this is what I and many others have suffered from the flute playing of this satyr. Yet hear me once more while I show you how exact the image is, and how marvellous his power. For let me tell you; none of you know him; but I will reveal him to you; having begun, I must go on. See you how fond he is of the fair? He is always with them and is always being smitten by them, and then again he knows nothing and is ignorant of all things—such is the appearance which he puts on. Is he not like a Silenus in this? To be sure he is: his outer mask is the carved head of the Silenus; but, O my companions in drink, when he is opened, what temperance there is residing within! Know you that beauty and wealth and honour, at which the many wonder, are of no account with him, and are utterly despised by him: he regards not at all the persons who are gifted with them; mankind are nothing to him; all his life is spent in mocking and flouting at them. But when I opened him, and looked within at his serious purpose, I saw in him divine and golden images of such fascinating beauty that I was ready to do in a moment whatever Socrates commanded: they may have escaped the observation of others, but I saw them. Now I fancied that he was seriously enamoured of my beauty, and I thought that I should therefore have a grand opportunity of hearing him tell what he knew, for I had a wonderful opinion of the attractions of my youth. In the prosecution of this design, when I next went to him, I sent away the attendant who usually accompanied me (I will confess the whole truth, and beg you to listen; and if I speak falsely, do you, Socrates, expose the falsehood). Well, he and I were alone together, and I thought that when there was nobody with us, I should hear him speak the language which lovers use to their loves when they are by themselves, and I was delighted. Nothing of the sort; he conversed as usual, and spent the day with me and then went away. Afterwards I challenged him to the palaestra; and he wrestled and closed with me several times when there was no one present; I fancied that I might succeed in this manner. Not a bit; I made no way with him. Lastly, as I had failed hitherto, I thought that I must take stronger measures and attack him boldly, and, as I had begun, not give him up, but see how matters stood between him and me. So I invited him to sup with me, just as if he were a fair youth, and I a designing lover. He was not easily persuaded to come; he did, however, after a while accept the invitation, and when he came the first time, he wanted to go away at once as soon as supper was over, and I had not the face to detain him. The second time, still in pursuance of my design, after we had supped, I went on conversing far into the night, and when he wanted to go away, I pretended that the hour was late and that he had much better remain. So he lay down on the couch next to me, the same on which he had supped, and there was no one but ourselves sleeping in the apartment. All this may be told without shame to any one. But what follows I could hardly tell you if I were sober. Yet as the proverb says, 'In vino veritas,' whether with boys, or without them (In allusion to two proverbs.); and therefore I must speak. Nor, again, should I be justified in concealing the lofty actions of Socrates when I come to praise him. Moreover I have felt the serpent's sting; and he who has suffered, as they say, is willing to tell his fellow-sufferers only, as they alone will be likely to understand him, and will not be extreme in judging of the sayings or doings which have been wrung from his agony. For I have been bitten by a more than viper's tooth; I have known in my soul, or in my heart, or in some other part, that worst of pangs, more violent in ingenuous youth than any serpent's tooth, the pang of philosophy, which will make a man say or do anything. And you whom I see around me, Phaedrus and Agathon and Eryximachus and Pausanias and Aristodemus and Aristophanes, all of you, and I need not say Socrates himself, have had experience of the same madness and passion in your longing after wisdom. Therefore listen and excuse my doings then and my sayings now. But let the attendants and other profane and unmannered persons close up the doors of their ears.

When the lamp was put out and the servants had gone

away, I thought that I must be plain with him and have no more ambiguity. So I gave him a shake, and I said: 'Socrates, are you asleep?' 'No,' he said. 'Do you know what I am meditating? 'What are you meditating?' he said. 'I think,' I replied, 'that of all the lovers whom I have ever had you are the only one who is worthy of me, and you appear to be too modest to speak. Now I feel that I should be a fool to refuse you this or any other favour, and therefore I come to lay at your feet all that I have and all that my friends have, in the hope that you will assist me in the way of virtue, which I desire above all things, and in which I believe that you can help me better than any one else. And I should certainly have more reason to be ashamed of what wise men would say if I were to refuse a favour to such as you, than of what the world, who are mostly fools, would say of me if I granted it.' To these words he replied in the ironical manner which is so characteristic of him:—'Alcibiades, my friend, you have indeed an elevated aim if what you say is true, and if there really is in me any power by which you may become better; truly you must see in me some rare beauty of a kind infinitely higher than any which I see in you. And therefore, if you mean to share with me and to exchange beauty for beauty, you will have greatly the advantage of me; you will gain true beauty in return for appearance—like Diomede, gold in exchange for brass. But look again, sweet friend, and see whether you are not deceived in me. The mind begins to grow critical when the bodily eye fails, and it will be a long time before you get old.' Hearing this, I said: 'I have told you my purpose, which is quite serious, and do you consider what you think best for you and me.' 'That is good,' he said; 'at some other time then we will consider and act as seems best about this and about other matters.' Whereupon, I fancied that he was smitten, and that the words which I had uttered like arrows had wounded him, and so without waiting to hear more I got up, and throwing my coat about him crept under his threadbare cloak, as the time of year was winter, and there I lay during the whole night having this wonderful monster in my arms. This again, Socrates, will not be denied by you. And yet, notwithstanding all, he was so superior to my solicitations, so contemptuous and derisive and disdainful of my beauty—which really, as I fancied, had some attractions—hear, O judges; for judges you shall be of the haughty virtue of Socrates—nothing more happened, but in the morning when I awoke (let all the gods and goddesses be my witnesses) I arose as from the couch of a father or an elder brother.

What do you suppose must have been my feelings, after this rejection, at the thought of my own dishonour? And yet I could not help wondering at his natural temperance and self-restraint and manliness. I never imagined that I could have met with a man such as he is in wisdom and endurance. And therefore I could not be angry with him or renounce his company, any more than I could hope to win him. For I well knew that if Ajax could not be wounded by steel, much less he by money; and my only chance of captivating him by my personal attractions had failed. So I was at my wit's end; no one was ever more hopelessly enslaved by another. All this happened before he and I went on the expedition to Potidaea; there we messed together, and I had the opportunity of observing his extraordinary power of sustaining fatigue. His endurance was simply marvellous when, being cut off from our supplies, we were compelled to go without food—on such occasions, which often happen in time of war, he was superior not only to me but to everybody; there was no one to be compared to him. Yet at a festival he was the only person who had any real powers of enjoyment; though not willing to drink, he could if compelled beat us all at that,—wonderful to relate! no human being had ever seen Socrates drunk; and his powers, if I am not mistaken, will be tested before long. His fortitude in enduring cold was also surprising. There was a severe frost, for the winter in that region is really tremendous, and everybody else either remained indoors, or if they went out had on an amazing quantity of clothes, and were well shod, and had their feet swathed in felt and fleeces: in the midst of this, Socrates with his bare feet on the ice and in his ordinary dress marched better than the other soldiers who had shoes, and they looked daggers at him because he seemed to despise them.

I have told you one tale, and now I must tell you another, which is worth hearing,

'Of the doings and sufferings of the enduring man'

while he was on the expedition. One morning he was thinking about something which he could not resolve; he would not give it up, but continued thinking from early dawn until noon—there he stood fixed in thought; and at noon attention was drawn to him, and the rumour ran through the wondering crowd that Socrates had been standing and thinking about something ever since the break of day. At last, in the evening after supper, some Ionians out of curiosity (I should explain that this was not in winter but in summer), brought out their mats and slept in the open air that they might watch him and see whether he would stand all night. There he stood until the following morning; and with the return of light he offered up a prayer to the sun, and went his way (compare supra). I will also tell, if you please—and indeed I am bound to tell—of his courage in battle; for who but he saved my life? Now this was the engagement in which I received the prize of valour: for I was wounded and he would not leave me, but he rescued me and my arms; and he ought to have received the prize of valour which the generals wanted to confer on me partly on account of my rank, and I told them so, (this, again, Socrates will not impeach or deny), but he was more eager than the generals that I and not he should have the prize. There was another occasion on which his behaviour was very remarkable—in the flight of the army after the battle of Delium, where he served among the heavy-armed,—I had a better opportunity of seeing him than at Potidaea, for I was myself on horseback, and therefore comparatively out of danger. He and Laches were retreating, for the troops were in flight, and I met them and told them not to be discouraged, and promised to remain with them; and there you might see him, Aristophanes, as you describe (Aristoph. Clouds), just as he is in the streets of Athens, stalking like a pelican, and rolling his eyes, calmly contemplating enemies as well as friends, and making very intelligible to anybody, even from a distance, that whoever attacked him would be likely to meet with a stout resistance; and in this way he and his companion escaped—for this is the sort of man who is never touched in war; those only are pursued who are running away headlong. I particularly observed how superior he was to Laches in presence of mind. Many are the marvels which I might narrate in praise of Socrates;

most of his ways might perhaps be paralleled in another man, but his absolute unlikeness to any human being that is or ever has been is perfectly astonishing. You may imagine Brasidas and others to have been like Achilles; or you may imagine Nestor and Antenor to have been like Pericles; and the same may be said of other famous men, but of this strange being you will never be able to find any likeness, however remote, either among men who now are or who ever have been—other than that which I have already suggested of Silenus and the satyrs; and they represent in a figure not only himself, but his words. For, although I forgot to mention this to you before, his words are like the images of Silenus which open; they are ridiculous when you first hear them; he clothes himself in language that is like the skin of the wanton satyr—for his talk is of pack-asses and smiths and cobblers and curriers, and he is always repeating the same things in the same words (compare Gorg.), so that any ignorant or inexperienced person might feel disposed to laugh at him; but he who opens the bust and sees what is within will find that they are the only words which have a meaning in them, and also the most divine, abounding in fair images of virtue, and of the widest comprehension, or rather extending to the whole duty of a good and honourable man.

This, friends, is my praise of Socrates. I have added my blame of him for his ill-treatment of me; and he has ill-treated not only me, but Charmides the son of Glaucon, and Euthydemus the son of Diocles, and many others in the same way—beginning as their lover he has ended by making them pay their addresses to him. Wherefore I say to you, Agathon, 'Be not deceived by him; learn from me and take warning, and do not be a fool and learn by experience, as the proverb says.'

When Alcibiades had finished, there was a laugh at his outspokenness; for he seemed to be still in love with Socrates. You are sober, Alcibiades, said Socrates, or you would never have gone so far about to hide the purpose of your satyr's praises, for all this long story is only an ingenious circumlocution, of which the point comes in by the way at the end; you want to get up a quarrel between me and Agathon, and your notion is that I ought to love you and nobody else, and that you and you only ought to love Agathon. But the plot of this Satyric or Silenic drama has been detected, and you must not allow him, Agathon, to set us at variance.

I believe you are right, said Agathon, and I am disposed to think that his intention in placing himself between you and me was only to divide us; but he shall gain nothing by that move; for I will go and lie on the couch next to you.

Yes, yes, replied Socrates, by all means come here and lie on the couch below me.

Alas, said Alcibiades, how I am fooled by this man; he is determined to get the better of me at every turn. I do beseech you, allow Agathon to lie between us.

Certainly not, said Socrates, as you praised me, and I in turn ought to praise my neighbour on the right, he will be out of order in praising me again when he ought rather to be praised by me, and I must entreat you to consent to this, and not be jealous, for I have a great desire to praise the youth.

Hurrah! cried Agathon, I will rise instantly, that I may be praised by Socrates.

The usual way, said Alcibiades; where Socrates is, no one else has any chance with the fair; and now how readily has he invented a specious reason for attracting Agathon to himself.

Agathon arose in order that he might take his place on the couch by Socrates, when suddenly a band of revellers entered, and spoiled the order of the banquet. Some one who was going out having left the door open, they had found their way in, and made themselves at home; great confusion ensued, and every one was compelled to drink large quantities of wine. Aristodemus said that Eryximachus, Phaedrus, and others went away—he himself fell asleep, and as the nights were long took a good rest: he was awakened towards daybreak by a crowing of cocks, and when he awoke, the others were either asleep, or had gone away; there remained only Socrates, Aristophanes, and Agathon, who were drinking out of a large goblet which they passed round, and Socrates was discoursing to them. Aristodemus was only half awake, and he did not hear the beginning of the discourse; the chief thing which he remembered was Socrates compelling the other two to acknowledge that the genius of comedy was the same with that of tragedy, and that the true artist in tragedy was an artist in comedy also. To this they were constrained to assent, being drowsy, and not quite following the argument. And first of all Aristophanes dropped off, then, when the day was already dawning, Agathon. Socrates, having laid them to sleep, rose to depart; Aristodemus, as his manner was, following him. At the Lyceum he took a bath, and passed the day as usual. In the evening he retired to rest at his own home.